Hassan Vali Nasab

Risk Assessment in Sustainability of Dredging Projects

Hassan Vali Nasab

Risk Assessment in Sustainability of Dredging Projects

by Considering Uncertainties

Noor Publishing

Imprint

Any brand names and product names mentioned in this book are subject to trademark, brand or patent protection and are trademarks or registered trademarks of their respective holders. The use of brand names, product names, common names, trade names, product descriptions etc. even without a particular marking in this work is in no way to be construed to mean that such names may be regarded as unrestricted in respect of trademark and brand protection legislation and could thus be used by anyone.

Cover image: www.ingimage.com

Publisher:
Noor Publishing
is a trademark of
Dodo Books Indian Ocean Ltd. and OmniScriptum S.R.L publishing group

120 High Road, East Finchley, London, N2 9ED, United Kingdom
Str. Armeneasca 28/1, office 1, Chisinau MD-2012, Republic of Moldova, Europe
Printed at: see last page
ISBN: 978-620-5-63431-8

Risk Assessment in Sustainability of Dredging Projects by Considering Uncertainties

By

Hassan Vali Nasab

Master's Student in Project and Construction Management, Alborz Non-Profit Institute, Iran

Dedicated to the merciful angels who:

The lord of the worlds, who began to guide his servants with the teaching of the pen.

My parents, whose presence is a crown of honor for me and their name is a reason for my existence because these two existences after the lord, have been the source of my existence, took my hand and taught me to walk in this valley full of ups and downs.

Content

Abstract

Excavation projects in urban areas are encountered with some problems. Thus the engineers should consider an appropriate margin of safety for design and construction. Conventional methods of slope stability analysis are usually based on limit state analysis and factor of safety criterion. These methods do not take into account the uncertainties. It is attempted to utilize the risk based approaches to overcome those deficiencies. In this approach, the safety factor is determined based on the parameters pertinent to uncertainties and level of acceptable risk. These methods can be used to evaluate the risk of failure and the necessary measures to control the risks. Monte Carlo simulation method is a probabilistic assessment tools to quantify the uncertainties. In the present research, slope stability of nailed wall has been investigated utilizing Monte Carlo simulation and the reliability index and probability of failure has been computed.

Key words: Excavation, Uncertainty, Risk Assessment, Monte Carlo Simulation, Nailing, Reliability Analysis.

Chapter I

Introduction

Introduction

With the growth of the population, the need for construction increases, and this is only possible with the expansion of civil infrastructures. On the other hand, the lack of high-quality land (land whose soil has suitable mechanical properties for construction) in densely populated cities, as well as the high cost of land in some areas, has led to the expansion of construction below the ground level. In some cases, due to the presence of obstacles such as the existence of buildings and underground facilities in the neighboring properties, excavations are carried out vertically.

It is obvious that in order to prevent possible accidents, excavation operations must be accompanied by stabilization. If the appropriate safety factor is not included in the design of the excavation wall stabilization, it can cause irreparable human and financial losses. The occasional news of nearby buildings toppling during excavation shows the risk-taking and importance of this issue. On the other hand, the factors that are involved in determining the confidence factor also have uncertainty, in the sense that by changing each of these factors, the confidence factor is also changed, as a result, the risk tolerance and risk probability also change. If this issue is ignored in the designs, it can impose unwanted costs. It should be noted that very large reliability coefficients also increase stabilization costs.

Therefore, in addition to the safety aspects, the accurate and informed estimation of the reliability factor can also reduce the cost of these projects from an economic point of view. Deep excavation on the Nicol Expressway in Singapore is an example of a massive geotechnical project that led to disaster a few years ago. This excavation was being carried out at a depth of 30 meters and with a width of 10 to 15 meters in Marni clay, with the bracing of the diaphragm wall, and on the afternoon of April 20, 2004, the wind beam above it broke, resulting in a 110-meter land fall. Which caused the collapse of Nicol highway in that area?

Also, the large movement of soil caused an explosion in the gas supply pipes and a fire. 4 people died in this incident. Unfortunately, in recent years, similar incidents have happened in our dear country, Iran. The expansion of excavations and the possibility of such incidents show the importance of this issue.

The analysis of geotechnical structures based on risk assessment is a topic that has recently attracted the attention of researchers. The reason for this approach is the existence of non-deterministic parameters or uncertainties in geotechnical issues. Because the existence of uncertainties leads to unsafe designs. Therefore, the degree of uncertainty of the design and the risks caused by this design should be evaluated in order to reduce the amount of damages by risk management. Risk management is the systematic application of management procedures, practices and policies to identify, analyze, evaluate, reduce and monitor risk. Risk reduction is the use of appropriate methods and management principles to reduce the probability of an event or its adverse consequences or both. Risk estimation and its comparison with acceptance criteria (quantitative or qualitative) is an integral part of risk management.

Statement of the research topic

Researchers have always sought to quantify phenomena and use probabilistic theories to model and analyze them. The quantification of phenomena and the use of probability theories were considered in the 16th and 17th centuries. The issue of risk and its management was also raised a few years after that and it quickly received attention in various sciences, but its current form was raised after 1960, which led to the emergence of insurance. The principles of risk assessment and management have been applied more formally to urban areas at risk of landslides and slope control around highways since the 1970s. In the 1980s, and especially in the 1990s, with the introduction of quantitative methods, pipeline route risk management and especially slope risk management developed.

Many researchers such as Warrens (1984), Whitman (1984), Einstein (1988, 1997), Fell (1994), Leroy (1996), Wu et al. (1996), Fell and Hartford (1997), Nadim and Lacasse (1999) Hu et al. (2000) Waltsed et al. (2001), Nadeem et al. (2003), Nadeem and Lacasse (2003, 2004), Hartford and Beecher (2004), and Lee and Jones (2004) have played a role in this development. Recently, studies have been conducted with the aim of improving risk factors, emphasizing the importance of uncertainty analysis and validating probabilistic methods as a useful tool for decision making. One of the important features in risk assessment is that subsequent decisions are facilitated by analyzing different risk modes (for example, cost-benefit analysis). This research explains how to use probabilistic methods to describe uncertainty and assess risk as an analytical tool for decision making.

Design based on risk assessment

As mentioned, all engineering designs face uncertainty. Uncertainty is evident in material specifications, operating conditions, engineering models, and so on. In fact, due to these uncertainties, geotechnical engineers consider the design capacity more than the required value of the project. The ratio of capacity to demand (reliability factor) is usually chosen based on experience. This method has major drawbacks. For example, this method is conservative. As a result, the overconfidence factor in the design is unknown. Although conservatism in estimating soil characteristics and forces seems reasonable. Due to the variety of uncertainties, a fixed confidence factor in different problems leads to different failure probabilities. The design based on risk assessment can cover some of the limitations of the certainty factor. Design based on risk assessment means trying to quantify the inherent uncertainties of an engineering problem and how to deal with them.

"Design based on risk assessment" in geotechnical engineering is divided into two parts: Data analysis and model structure. In the data analysis part, uncertainties are identified and quantified using statistical relationships. In the model building phase, mathematical relationships are used to evaluate the effect of uncertainties in calculations. Another result of risk-based design is quantifying the reliability of the structure. This value is called "Reliability index".

Comparison of traditional methods and probabilistic methods

The piedra analysis of the slopes is traditionally based on determining the reliability coefficient. Geotechnical experts rely heavily on empirical judgments, such as the concept of confidence factor, to assess the stability of a suitable slope for development. The reliability coefficient of slopes is defined as the ratio of the shear capacity at the critical failure level to the shear stress applied to that level. In other words, the reliability factor measures the ratio of resistance that must be reduced so that the slope reaches the definite failure point. Recently, it has been found that the value of the confidence factor does not necessarily predict good slope stability performance.

One of the limitations of using the confidence factor is the existence of uncertainties in soil resistance parameters. If it is possible to define the variability of the stability analysis input parameters such as adhesion, friction angle and soil specific gravity in the form of probability density, the confidence coefficient of the slope will also follow a probability density. New methods of dam safety are available that can assist geotechnical engineers in quantifying uncertainties affecting slope stability. In these methods, both numerical methods and reasonable judgments are used to quantify the uncertainties or risks in a system such as a slope and are presented in a reference format called Quantitative Risk Assessment (QRA).

The purpose and scope of the research

In designs, the balance between safety and construction cost should be considered. It is possible to have an accurate design only if we have an accurate prediction of its performance, but since in reality such prediction accuracy is not accessible, as a result, a margin of safety must be considered. This margin of confidence is often included in the form of increasing the confidence factor. Increasing the reliability factor means more conservative design and more costs. Therefore, reliability cannot be considered as an ideal criterion for high importance projects. Because the reliability coefficient is expressed as an exact number and any implementation issues and uncertainties in the soil are not included in it.

An analysis with a higher confidence factor may be more likely to fail than an analysis with a lower confidence factor. Also, the reliability factor cannot justify the probability of failure and its consequences. However, economic benefits can be expressed using risk methods as the basis for design, because this method enables the optimization of at least the part of the design that is related to uncertainties. Optimal design is based on maintaining a balance between risk and cost.

However, an increase in conservatism leads to a decrease in the probability of improper performance of the structure. At the same time, it increases the cost of construction. A degree of conservatism where an increase in construction cost results in a significant reduction in risk can be cost-effective. As a result, creating a balance between existing risks, costs and benefits is considered one of the basic discussions of risk management. The purpose of this research is to assess the risk of excavation projects in order to create a balance between existing risks, costs and benefits by taking advantage of the relationship between the probability of failure and the performance level of the structure.

Thesis structure

This research can be generally divided into three parts: Stability methods and well analysis, management of uncertainty sources, and methods of capability analysis and risk assessment. In this study, first, the technical literature related to risk assessment methods is examined. In the next step, different pit stabilization methods have been introduced and compared. And finally, by defining the effective uncertainties in pit stabilization as well as the existing processes of risk assessment, it will be investigated how to perform the analysis for a specific risk, i.e. pit instability risk. The second chapter of this thesis deals with a review of the subject literature. In this chapter, stabilization methods are first introduced, then common well stability analysis methods are briefly described.

In the third chapter, management of uncertainty sources, risk-based methods and reliability analysis methods are discussed. In this chapter, after reviewing the methods of quantifying the uncertainties, the concepts of risk management in the pit are briefly explained, then the characteristics and concepts of the probability analysis of the stability of the slopes and the relevant calculation theory, including the Monte Carlo simulation method, which is discussed in this thesis has been used and paid for.

The fourth chapter of this thesis deals with the study of probabilistic analysis of pit wall stability by mentioning an example. In this chapter, according to the material presented in previous chapters, the probabilistic analysis of pit stability by SLOPE/W software is discussed and investigated.

The fifth chapter of this thesis deals with the final summary and offers suggestions for further research based on the studies conducted in this thesis.

Chapter II

A Review of the Thematic Literature on Well Analysis and Stabilization Methods

In recent years, with the increase in density and the number of floors and the need to provide parking and other service levels in buildings, the depth of excavation has also increased. Therefore, with the increase of excavation depth, the risks of instability and rupture of excavation walls increase greatly. Excavation generally refers to an act in which soil or rock is removed from a place by machines or explosives and is made into an open face, hole or pit.

A safe well is a well that is sufficiently stable and not exposed to unacceptable risks. Contrary to the opinion of some people who think that the use of necessary safety measures in excavation imposes unnecessary cost and time, excavation is considered to be one of the most complex and dangerous engineering works, and especially in deeper pits, it requires comprehensive investigations, precision and Monitoring and ultimately spending considerable time and money is necessary so that people's lives and property are not endangered in this way. However, lack of familiarity with technical principles, negligence or irresponsible profit-seeking leads to accidents.

The pits that are created in the vicinity of the existing buildings should not damage the stability of these buildings in any way, either in the implementation phase or in the exploitation phase. As a result of deep excavations, public safety has been jeopardized and we have witnessed the rupture of excavation walls and the occurrence of financial and life damages to workers, neighbors, passers-by, as well as traffic restrictions in the passages adjacent to the excavation. Therefore, in order to design the stability of excavation walls, it must be ensured that there is a sufficient safety factor for the life of the stabilizing structures.

Excavation, especially deep excavations, disrupts the balance of the soil and changes the state of stresses in the soil. Also, as a result of excavation operations, there are deformations in the soil that cause soil cohesion or soil rupture, or cause the balance and stability of the structure adjacent to the pit to be disturbed. Necessities that lead to excavation operations include: building a basement, building a parking lot, land restrictions in cities and ever-increasing land prices, building a canal, creating a trench, etc.

The division of pits according to depth H is as follows

Shallow H < 6m

Deep H > 6m

The design of both types of pits is similar and is done based on the theories of soil and structure mechanics.

The lateral pressure on the pit wall is due to the weight of the adjacent soil mass or the loads on it. This overhead can be due to the weight of nearby buildings or the use of nearby roads. If the forces on the pit wall are greater than the soil resistance, the pit wall will collapse. To ensure the safety of the trenches during excavation, these projects must be evaluated and calculated, and if the reliability factor is lower than the expected value, in order to prevent the trench from falling and the possible negative consequences caused by this excavation, temporary structures should be installed. They perform to control the trench, which are called guarding structures. In the following, while introducing the guard structures used for pit stability, we will also review some slope stability analysis methods.

Conventional methods of excavation and buffer construction

If it is determined after performing the calculations that the soil alone cannot withstand the lateral pressures, it should be stabilized by constructing suitable guarding structures for the pit wall. Guard structures are temporary structures that are implemented to contain the trench.

The main objectives of securing the pit wall using guard structures are:
- ➢ Preservation of human lives inside and outside the pit;
- ➢ Keeping property inside and outside the pit;
- ➢ Providing safe and secure conditions for the execution of work.

Conventional excavation and buffering methods are:

➢ Slope excavation;

➢ Excavation with a nailed wall (Rock Bolt, shotcrete, etc.);

➢ Excavation using the method of improving soil properties (freezing, injection, etc.);

➢ Excavation using retaining structures.

Pit stabilization methods

Every year, different countries spend a lot of money on domain stability. Depending on the geometric conditions of the domain, the size of the unstable mass, the resistance characteristics of the soil, the location and location of the domain, etc., there are various methods for stabilizing the gables. Each of these methods can be used in stabilization according to the situation and conditions of projects. The most important factor in choosing a sustainability method is to achieve maximum sustainability with the lowest cost, and of course, the location and conditions of the project are also determining factors in choosing the sustainability method.

The appropriate excavation method according to the type of soil, underground water level, depth of the pit and the location and conditions of the neighbors and the legal requirements of the construction and especially the people, stabilization costs (initial costs, implementation costs, collection costs of the temporary structure), costs due to damage (rupture and or shape change) and implementation problems and limitations are selected. Pit stabilization methods were formed simultaneously with the feeling of human need for construction under the surface of the earth, the simplest of which is creating a stable slope on the excavation surface. With the passage of time and the creation of basic limitations, such as the lack of space to create a suitable slope for the pit, engineers thought of ways to deal with the fall of vertical soil surfaces. Early methods to deal with spillage that are still used such as piles, horizontal and inclined supports, Berlin walls and trusses were invented and were added to them with the thoughtful innovations of reinforced soil and nailing.

The importance of using these methods becomes more obvious when looking at the destroyed examples of new and old buildings and structures in the vicinity of unprincipled excavations. Many human and financial damages that have occurred due to the non-compliance of engineering principles in excavation and also the failure to use the proper pit protection method will never be compensated. Therefore, it is inevitable to investigate and identify different methods of creating guard structures and the basic application of these methods. Types of pit stabilization methods are:

- ❖ Anchorage;
- ❖ Sewing on the back (pinning) (Tie back);
- ❖ Diaphragm Wall;
- ❖ Reciprocal Support;
- ❖ Piling;
- ❖ Sheet Piling;
- ❖ Truss construction;
- ❖ Micro pile method;
- ❖ Nailing method.

Also, the methods of stabilizing excavation walls can be divided into the following two general categories:

Providing stability from inside the pit

In excavations where, due to technical or legal reasons, it is not possible to create a wall on the sides of the building without providing proper support for it, and it is not possible to expect that the wall itself will be static, stabilization of the excavation wall from inside the origin is inevitable. Facing restraint methods, trusses, diaphragms and in-situ piling are among the methods of providing stability from inside the pit. In cases where it is necessary to limit the horizontal deformations in the excavation wall, the most suitable method for shallow excavations is the facing restraint method and in other cases the truss method or combined methods.

Ensuring the stability of the excavation wall from outside the pit

In cases where the stability of the excavation wall can be provided by creating a slope or digging on the sides of the origin within the scope of ownership or obtaining permission from the owners of the adjacent properties, the methods of stabilizing the excavation wall from outside the pit are considered. Anchoring methods, pile and anchoring, diaphragm wall and anchoring and nailing are the methods of stabilizing the excavation wall from outside the pit. In cases where there are limitations for the complete stabilization of the pit wall using one method, it is possible to provide the desired stability with the help of other methods and in a consolidated manner.

Factors affecting the selection of excavation methods

Stabilization methods of pit walls according to the condition and type of soil, excavation depth, dimensions of the pit, underground water level, location and manner of pit location, seismicity of the area, control and supervision of the responsible organizations, insurance coverage and most importantly the thinking and attitude of those involved matter of building is chosen for the rights and health of others and their risk tolerance.

Choosing each of these methods or a combination of them depends on various parameters, including the following:

- ❖ Volume of work;
- ❖ The depth of the pit;
- ❖ Location conditions of the project: A- Inside the city or outside it B- Congestion or solitude of the project environment;
- ❖ The location around the project: A- Waste land and its possible use B- The road and its width C- The building and its number of floors;
- ❖ The slope of the land; Available machinery;
- ❖ Available human resources;
- ❖ Administrative and technical rules and regulations;
- ❖ Economic conditions.

Causes of rupture in deep excavations

In general, the causes of excavation spillage are categorized as follows:

Open planting

➤ Lack of geotechnical studies, inappropriate selection of soil and rock parameters and underground water conditions.

➤ The designer's inattention to the effect of settlement on nearby buildings.

➤ The lack of understanding of the designer and contractor about the effects of weathering and time on the shear strength of the soil.

Excavation with structural elements

➤ Lack of geotechnical studies, inappropriate selection of soil and rock resistance parameters and underground water conditions.

➤ Inappropriate quality of structural details.

➤ Inconsistency between designer and contractor.

➤ The designer's ignorance of the limitations of specific methods of containment, stabilization, such as high-pressure injection and...

➤ The designer's inattention to the effect of shape changes in structural systems that hold soil and soil mass.

➤ Change in loading from conventional conditions such as water fluctuations, temperature and contractor's inattention to the effect of these factors.

➤ Changing the geotechnical conditions of soil and rock and the contractor's inattention to its effect on stability.

➤ Temporary unconventional loadings on soil buffer systems.

➤ Low quality of executive agents in carrying out partial activities.

Comparing the cost of implementing different well stabilization systems

Figure (1) shows the total cost of implementing ten different systems per square meter of stabilization, implemented in the United States in 2001. During the investigations, it was found that the nailing system can be effective in reducing costs by 10-30% (Sabatini et al, 1997). Of course, it should be noted that for different regions and times, different results may be obtained. On the other hand, due to the limitations of urban environments, systems number 1 to 5 are not very effective in urban areas.

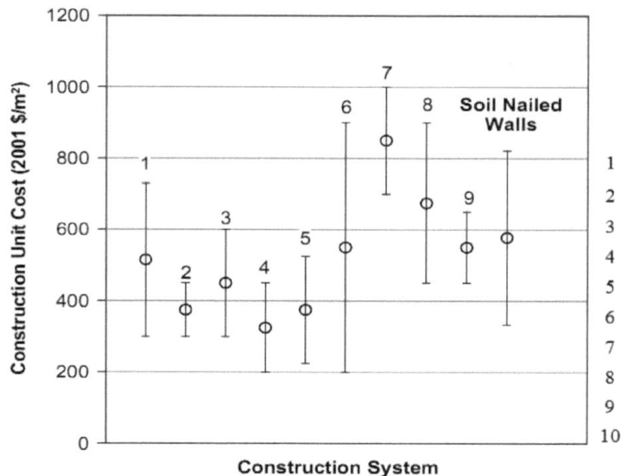

Figure 1. Comparing the cost of implementing different well stabilization systems

Depending on the presence or absence of underground water, cheap and competitive methods in urban environments are divided into two categories:

With a lot of underground water
- ➢ Deep soil mixing;
- ➢ High pressure injection columns;
- ➢ Diaphragm wall;
- ➢ Overlapping candles.

Without underground water or with little and drainable water

- ➢ Nailing;
- ➢ A separate candle with a harness and inner cover;
- ➢ Block with harness.

Pit stability analysis methods

The stability of pits is one of the issues that have been discussed since the past. Pit stability analysis is usually done to evaluate the safety of natural slopes, excavations, earthworks, earthen dams, excavations, etc. Along with the progress of pit stabilization methods in recent years, the stability analysis of pit wall has also made progress and over time they have changed the procedure from doing manual calculations to computer solutions and probabilistic analyses. In the following, the slope stability analysis methods are examined.

Traditional and conventional methods of pit stability analysis

Today, there are many methods to evaluate the safety of natural slopes, excavations, earthworks, earthen dams, etc., the most common of which is the use of force and anchor balance equations in the range of wedge rupture, as well as the use of the concept of confidence factor. The limit equilibrium method is the most important method, the basis of which is the solution of force and anchor balance equations. Solving these equations was very complicated and time-consuming in some cases. The complexity of the equations and the time-consuming calculations led the researchers to consider assumptions and simplifications for the ease of calculations. In this way, the difference in assumptions caused many limit equilibrium methods to be introduced for slope stability analysis over the years.

Among these methods, we can mention the usual method (Flenius, 1936), the modified method of Bishop (1955), Janbo method (1968), Morgenstern-Price method (1965) and Spencer method (1967). The general framework of these methods is the same despite the differences in the analysis process and the obtained results, and their theoretical basis is the use of vertical pieces cut from the sliding surface of Shirvani, and each method analyzes the stability of the piece according to its own hypotheses and principles. based on torque and force balances, as well as how horizontal (shear) and vertical forces affect the calculation process.

In the limit method, the stability of the slope is measured by the coefficient of confidence, which is expressed as the ratio between the shear strength of the soil and the shear stress required for equilibrium. The limit equilibrium methods are stable, which are often very useful for preliminary or preliminary analysis and rapid estimation of slope stability. One of the simplifications made in the analysis of the stability of the roofs is related to the shape of the sliding surface. Usually, the shape of the sliding surface is considered to be flat, circular or non-circular.

Considering that at the moment of rupture, the shear resistance is mobilized along the entire length of the slip surface, therefore, the shape of the slip surface must also be selected before starting the analysis.

The process of this analysis continues until the critical rupture level that has the lowest confidence coefficient. Many studies have been done to investigate the accuracy of some limit equilibrium methods and also to find a method to find the critical slip surface. Research has shown that in most cases, the assumption of the circularity of the sliding surface is very close to the results when the non-circular sliding surface is considered. With the difference that the assumption of circularity is very useful in reducing the volume of calculations related to the confidence factor, as a result, the critical slip surface can be assumed to be a circle in most cases, unless the layers of the earth that surround the slip surface are placed in a way that creates a surface become non-circular slip (Duncan, 1996).

General limit equilibrium method

General limit equilibrium is a general method that has most of the assumptions used in different methods and can analyze circular and non-circular sliding surfaces. This method is the framework and basis for other available methods to analyze the stability of earthen roofs. In this method, the sliding surface of Shirvani is divided into a series of vertical parts using vertical cuts, and the balance and stability of each part is provided based on the weight force and the forces acting on the part, including the forces between the parts and their torque. Therefore, this method can be considered as a method based on the balance of forces and their torque, and based on this and using Spencer's theory, the separate equations of the safety factor can be concluded from it. In this method, equations 1 and 2 are used to determine the safety factor based on the balance of forces and torque, respectively:

$$1 \qquad F_f = \frac{\sum(c'.\beta.\cos\alpha + (N-u.\beta).\tan\varnothing'.\cos\alpha)}{\sum N.\sin\alpha - \sum D.\cos\omega}$$

$$2 \qquad F_m = \frac{\sum(c'.\beta.R + (N-u.\beta).\tan\varnothing'.R)}{\sum W.x - \sum N.f \pm \sum D.d}$$

In these relationships, c' is the effective adhesion of soil particles, $\varnothing'$ is the effective friction angle of the soil, u is the pore water pressure, N is the vertical force, W is the weight of the piece, D is the linear load, α is the slope of the piece and other unknowns such as β, ω, R, x, f, d are also geometrical parameters that are determined based on the way of cutting each part of the sliding surface of Shirvani.

Also, the vertical force of the piece (N) in equations 1 and 2 is defined as follows:

$$3 \qquad N = \frac{W + (X_R - X_L) - \dfrac{c'.\beta.\sin\alpha + u.\beta.\sin\alpha.\tan\varnothing'}{F}}{\cos\alpha + \dfrac{\sin\alpha.\tan\varnothing'}{F}}$$

Where X_R and X_L are shearing forces applied to the right and left direction of the part, respectively.

In the above relationship, when N is used in the torque balance equation, F is equal to F_m, and if N is used in the force balance equation, F will actually be F_f.

In this method, the use of the effect of shear forces in the stability analysis of the roof is actually derived from the Morgenstern-Price method, whose model is described as follows:

$$4 \qquad X = E.\lambda.f(x)$$

Where X is the shear force on the part, E is the vertical force on the part, λ is the percentage of the slope of the force on the part and (x) f is also a function of the forces that can take values between 0 and 1.

Figure (2) helps to better understand the concept of λ.

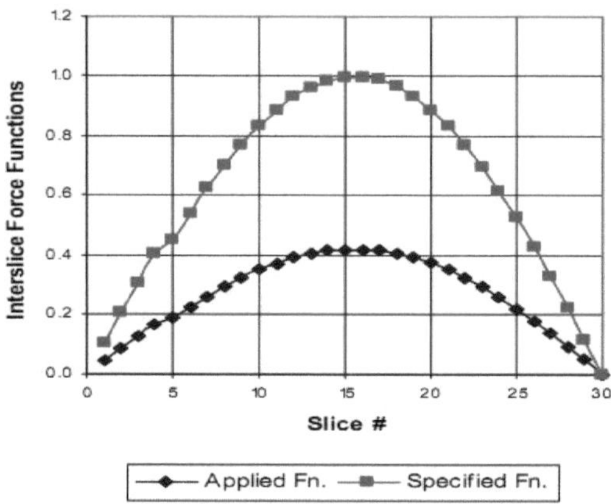

Figure 2. Diagram of changes in force function in an earthen terrace

In the above figure, the upper curve shows the theoretical force function and the lower curve shows the real force function. The ratio between these two curves is called λ, and in the above diagram, the value of λ is approximately equal to 0.43.

Flenius or normal method

This method, which is also referred to as the Swedish method, is one of the first methods that was introduced to manually calculate the stability coefficient of slopes. Since all internal forces are ignored in this method, its calculations are simpler. In this method, the confidence factor in the absence of pore water pressure and assuming the sliding surface is circular is expressed as the following relationship:

$$5 \qquad FS = \frac{\Sigma(c.\beta+N.\tan\emptyset)}{\Sigma W.\sin\alpha} = \frac{\Sigma S_{resistance}}{\Sigma S_{mobilized}}$$

Where: c adhesion, ϕ friction angle, β is the horizontal length of the wedge, α is the slope of the wedge, N is the vertical component of the weight, W is the weight of the wedge.

Bishop's simplified method

This method is based on torque balance, in which the effect of vertical forces is included in the stability analysis of the part, but the effect of horizontal (shear) forces is ignored in the stability analysis. In this method, the described model, unlike normal models, has repeated unknowns. The model used to determine the safety factor using the above method, in the absence of any pore water pressure, is described as follows:

$$6 \qquad FS = \frac{\sum\{c.\beta + W.\tan\emptyset\left[\cos\alpha + \frac{\sin\alpha.\tan\emptyset}{FS}\right]\}}{\sum W.\sin\alpha}$$

As you can see, FS parameter is on both sides of the equation. To solve this issue, a solution has also been provided, and based on this, another parameter called m_α is defined as follows:

$$7 \qquad m_\alpha = \cos\alpha + \frac{\sin\alpha.\tan\emptyset}{FS}$$

Therefore, to solve this problem, it is necessary to use the trial-and-error method. It is usually recommended to start solving this problem by assuming FS= 1 and having this hypothetical FS, the value of m_α is calculated and by placing it in the equation (6), a new FS is obtained. Now put this new FS again in relation (7) and another FS is obtained again. We continue this process until the last FS obtained has a slight difference with its previous value.

According to equation (4), to satisfy the conditions of Bishop's simplified method (absence of horizontal or vertical forces), it is necessary that the value of λ is equal to zero. Now, if we draw the graph of the changes of the confidence factor (FS) against λ (figure 3), it can be seen that the confidence factor of the simplified Bishop method is located on the torque balance curve and in a place where λ is equal to zero. (FS = 1.36) It is necessary to mention that the safety factor of the simplified Bishop method is placed on the torque balance curve because in this method the analysis of the stability of the parts is done only based on their torque balance.

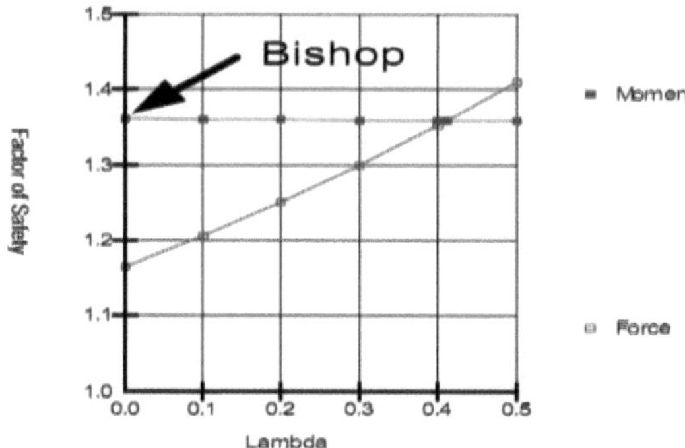

Figure 3. Chart of changes of FS in terms of λ and determination of confidence coefficient of Bishop's simplified method

The simplified method of Janbo

This method is similar to Bishop's simplified method, with the difference that in this method, only the force balance of the part is considered and the torque balance is not the criterion for analyzing the stability of the part. Ignoring the effect of shear forces of the part, the value of λ is taken as zero. Therefore, as seen in figure (4), the reliability coefficient of the simplified Janbo method is located on the force balance curve and in a place where the value of λ is zero. Therefore, the confidence coefficient of Janbo's simplified method (FS = 1.16) has a lower value than the confidence coefficient of Y bishop's simplified method (FS = 1.36).

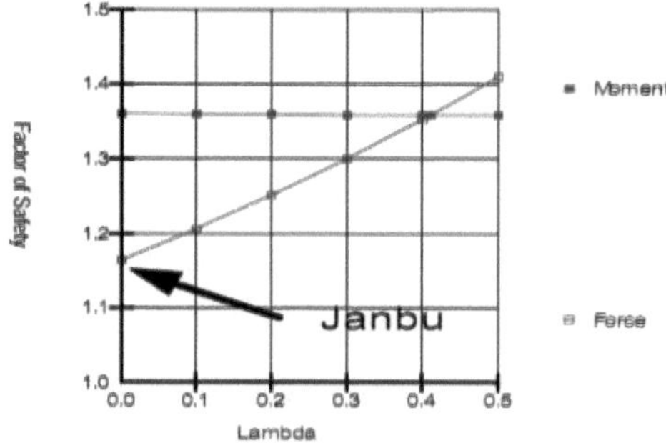

Figure 4. The graph of changes of FS in terms of λ and the determination of the reliability coefficient of the simplified Janbo method

Spencer method

Spencer stated this method based on two safety factor models, one based on the torque balance and the other based on the force balance on the part in 1967. In this method, the function (x)f is always considered a constant function and therefore, according to the model (x)f.E.λ=X, the ratio of the (horizontal) shearing force to the vertical force will be the same in all parts.

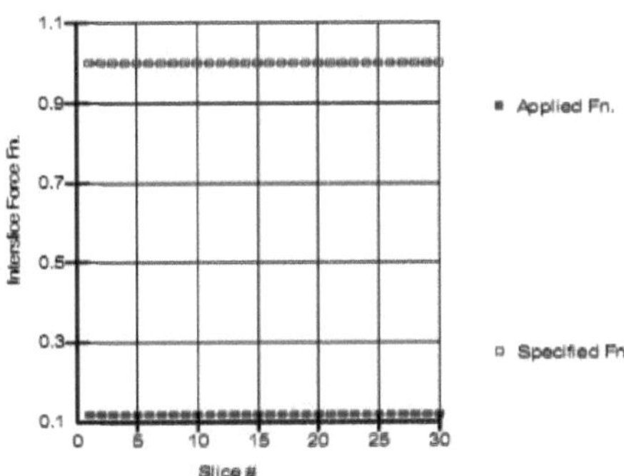

Figure 5. Chart of changes of force function in an earthen terrace

In figure (5), the upper diagram shows the theoretical force function and the lower diagram shows the real force function. The ratio between these two graphs is equal to λ, whose value in figure (5) is equal to 0.12. On the other hand, in this method, both the balance of torque and forces are provided, therefore, the reliability coefficient of this method is located in the intersection of the curves of torque and force balance in the graph of changes of FS versus λ according to figure 2-7.

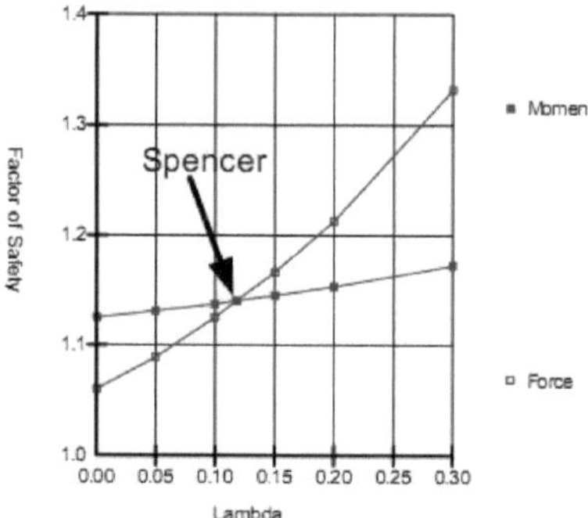

Figure 6. The diagram of FS changes in terms of λ and determination of Spencer's confidence coefficient

As can be seen, the intersection of the two curves is at λ=0.12, which is equal to its value in figure (6). Considering that in figure 2-6, we considered (x)f as a constant function, we will have:

$$\text{if } f(x)=1: X = E \times 0/12 \times 1 = 0/12 \text{ or } 0/12 = E/X$$

The ratio E/X = 0.12 means that the ratio of the shearing force on the right and left surfaces of each part of the sliding surface of the soil slope to the vertical force on the same surface is equal to 0.12. This ratio shows that the resultant force in the desired piece has an angle of Arctg (0.12) or 6.74 degrees with respect to the horizon.

Morgenstern-Price method

This method is similar to Spencer's method and is based on force balance and moment balance, with the difference that unlike Spencer's method which used only one constant function in the calculation of the stability balance of the earthen roof, this method can use f(x) functions.

But in other conditions, the Morgenstern-Price method is completely similar to the Spencer method. The graph of changes of the safety factor based on the balance of the torque of the forces relative to Landa (λ) is shown in figure (7). As can be seen, due to the use of both torque and force balance, the reliability factor of this method is located at the intersection of two curves.

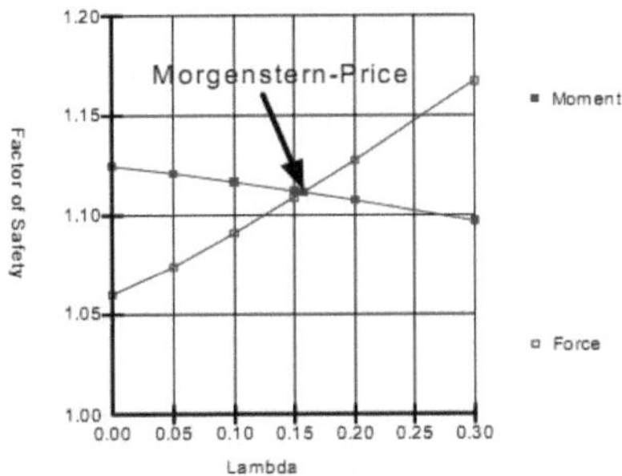

Figure 7. The diagram of FS changes in terms of λ and the determination of the confidence coefficient of the Morgenstern-Price method

The remarkable point is that the reliability coefficient of the Morgenstern-Price method has a lower value compared to the simplified Bishop method.

The method of the group of engineers

This method is not dependent on torque balance and is proposed only on the basis of force balance. Therefore, in this method, all horizontal (shear) and vertical forces are used in the stability analysis of the part. Using this method, the stability of the earthen roof is investigated from two perspectives:

❖ The first approach uses the slope of the connecting line between the top and the foot of the gable. From this point of view, this line shows the hypothetical direction of the descending force of Shirvani sliding surface. In other words, the direction of the descent force of the Shirvani sliding surface is parallel to the line drawn from the top to the bottom of the sliding surface.

❖ In the second view, the direction of the downward force is parallel to the slope of the earth's surface above the Shirvani slip surface. For example, if the slope of the upper surface of the roof is 2 horizontals to 1 vertical, then the ratio of the shear force to the vertical force of this sliding surface will be

29

0.5, or if the ground surface is horizontal, the direction of the downward force will also be horizontal and the ratio E/ X will be zero. In this method, unlike the Morgenstern-Price or Spencer method, there is no single value for λ and the value of λ will be the average of several values obtained based on the assumptions of this method.

Sarma method

In this method, a solution for analyzing the stability of different cutting modes of pieces has been presented. In this method, the pieces cut from the sliding surface of Shirvani can have any desired shape. But due to the difficulty of defining and specifying the cut geometric shape, usually only the vertical cut dimension of the pieces is used. In his method, Sarma presented a model similar to the Moore-Columb shear strength model for the relationship between the vertical and shear forces of the parts. This model is as follows:

$$8 \qquad tg\o.\, E + (h + c) = X$$

Where c is adhesion resistance, h is the height of the side of the piece and $\o$ is the internal friction angle of the soil.

To get suitable and acceptable results from the above model, it is better that the adhesion value (c) is zero or very small. Therefore, to use this method, we first assume that the amount of adhesion is zero, but in the continuation of the analysis, we can add a small amount to it. Of course, this work should be done with special care and attention and considering all aspects of the work. This method, like Spencer's method, uses both moment and force balance in stability analysis, and all vertical and horizontal (shear) forces are effective in Shirvani stability analysis.

Pit stability analysis by finite element method

One of the new methods used for slope stability analysis is the Finite Element Method (FEM). Compared to the limit equilibrium method, it has not been established yet (Duncan 1996; Griffiths and Lane 1999). The reason for this is that the limit equilibrium methods were theoretically simple and in computer programs they can obtain a suitable and quick estimate of the reliability coefficient, in contrast to the finite element method, which has a complex and time-consuming theory to model the parameters (Duncan 1996). However, the use of finite elements for slope stability analysis also has advantages over limit equilibrium methods. Some of these advantages are (Griffiths and Lane, 1999):

❖ No special assumption is needed for the position and shape of the sliding surface. Failure occurs in areas where the soil elements have less shear resistance than the applied shear stress.

❖ Contrary to some limit balance methods, the assumptions related to internal forces are the main source of error in them. The finite element method considers the overall equilibrium up to the moment of rupture, and no hypothesis about the internal forces is necessary.

❖ If the soil hardness parameters are correctly modeled, the finite element method provides information about the deformation caused by the stress before the moment of rupture.

❖ The finite element method is able to provide information about gradual failure up to the stage of overall shear failure.

❖ In recent years, many studies have been conducted regarding the use of finite element method for slope stability analysis. Among the researchers who have conducted studies in this field are Smith and Hobbs (1975), Griffiths (1980), Putz and his colleagues (1990), Matsui and Son (1992), Jermick (2000), Zheng and his colleagues (2006) and Lee (2007) pointed out. In addition, studies were conducted by Zinkevich and his colleagues (1975) and Griffiths (1980) to analyze the stability of slopes using the finite element method, which showed that the reliability coefficient calculated by the finite element method is in good agreement with the reliability coefficient of the limit equilibrium method.

Probability analysis methods of pit stability

Slope stability analysis is done with traditional methods in a certain framework. This means that the input parameters (such as resistance parameters) are based only on the best estimate obtained from the experiments. In most cases, when experimental data are limited, engineering judgment requires that past experience be used to obtain the best estimate for each parameter. This makes the calculated confidence factor not only dependent on the choice of analysis method and considered failure mode, but also on the uncertainty of the input parameters and the reliability of the assumptions.

Therefore, in traditional approaches, higher reliability coefficients are considered for the analysis and design of roofs. Today, it has been proven that the confidence factor alone is an ineffective tool for quantifying the uncertainty of soil characteristics (Duncan, 2000). Therefore, it seems necessary to have a suitable framework that can help to quantify the impact of uncertainties in well stability analysis. In this regard, probabilistic well stability analysis was proposed in the 1970s in order to quantify the impact of uncertainties. Wu and Croft (1970), Alonso (1976), Tang et al. (1976) and Wenmark (b1997) were among the first researchers who conducted studies in this field. Compared with deterministic analyses, probabilistic analyzes introduce uncertainties in the calculation parameters and instead of using the confidence factor in the safety level of the project, it usually uses the failure probability or confidence index. In these methods, large values of the reliability index indicate a safer well.

Probabilistic approaches can be divided into three general categories:

1- Approximate methods

- First-order verification method (FORM);
- First order second moment method (FOSM);
- Point estimation method (PEM).

2- Simulation methods

3- Mathematical methods

We will discuss these methods in detail in the next chapter.

Summary

According to the assumptions and simplifications made, each of the above methods have advantages and limitations, but the important and practical point is that by studying and examining each of these methods, one can gain a deep understanding of the method and its limitations. Each of them found and gained more confidence from the process of performing analysis and receiving more realistic confidence coefficients. In other words, the correct understanding of the methods and their advantages and limitations, makes us not to expect results beyond the capabilities of the methods in performing the analysis.

Below are the things that should be taken into account when choosing a method:

➢ In the analysis and determination of reliability coefficients of the stability of earthen roofs, due to the sensitivity and the need to pay more attention to the construction of various types of structures, it is recommended to use methods such as the Morgenstern-Price or Spencer method, which satisfy both torque and force balance and the overall effect forces acting on the parts, both horizontal (shear) and vertical forces are considered, so that the reliability coefficients obtained in real conditions can easily meet the stability requirement of the earthen roof.

➢ Morgenstern-Price or Spencer methods, due to considering the simultaneous effect of all forces, usually result in lower confidence coefficients and have a lower error percentage than other methods. It should be mentioned that the reliability coefficient value obtained based on Janbo and Bishop's methods, which satisfy only one of the force and torque balances, is about $\pm15\%$ different from the answers obtained by Morgenstern-Price and Spencer methods.

➢ The reliability coefficient obtained from the simplified Bishop method for circular sliding surfaces can differ by less than 5% with more accurate methods.

➢ Janbo's simplified method, which is generally used for non-circular surfaces, estimates the confidence factor to be less than the actual value, the difference of which is about 30% compared to more accurate methods.

The piedra analysis of the slopes is traditionally based on determining the reliability coefficient. Geotechnical experts rely heavily on empirical judgments, such as the concept of confidence factor, to assess the stability of a suitable slope for development. The reliability coefficient of slopes is defined as the ratio of the shear capacity at the critical failure level to the shear stress applied to that level. In other words, the reliability factor measures the ratio of resistance that must be reduced so that the slope reaches the definite failure point. Recently, it has been found that the value of the confidence factor does not necessarily predict good slope stability performance. One of the limitations of using the confidence factor is the existence of uncertainties in soil resistance parameters. If it is possible to define the variability of the stability analysis input parameters such as adhesion, friction angle and soil specific gravity in the form of probability density, the confidence coefficient of the slope will also follow a probability density. This issue is shown in figure (8) for two different slopes, due to the relative difference in the variability of the input parameters, two different density functions have been obtained for the confidence factor.

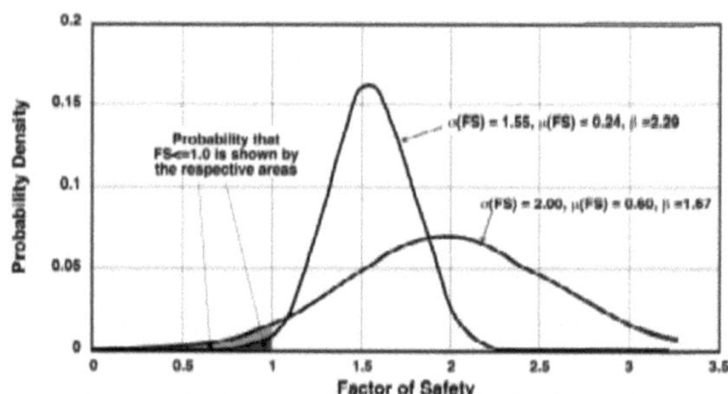

Figure 8. Different probability density for different confidence factor in slope stability

New methods of dam safety are available that can assist geotechnical engineers in quantifying uncertainties affecting slope stability. In these methods, both numerical methods and reasonable judgments are used to quantify the uncertainties or risks in a system such as a slope and are presented in a reference format called Quantitative Risk Assessment (QRA).

Chapter III

Management of Uncertainty Resources and Risk-Based Design

Introduction

Any construction project that includes excavation or is near a trench with a depth of more than 1.5 meters or a tunnel is known as a high-risk construction project. Regardless of the method of excavation, risks arising from site excavation must be managed. For high-risk excavations such as trenches, shafts and tunnels, special arrangements should be considered. If the appropriate safety factor is not included in the design of the excavation wall stabilization, it can cause irreparable human and financial losses. The occasional news of nearby buildings toppling during excavation shows the risk-taking and importance of this issue.

On the other hand, the factors that are involved in determining the reliability coefficient themselves also have uncertainty, in the sense that with the change of each of these factors, the reliability coefficient is also subject to change, as a result, the risk tolerance and risk probability also change. On the other hand, the selection of soil geotechnical parameters is one of the main stages of designing geotechnical structures, which is very complex and challenging due to the existing uncertainties.

Therefore, the best solution to include uncertainty in soil is to use soil characteristics in the form of non-deterministic analysis. Uncertainty analysis includes methods that consider the effect of uncertainty in the input parameters and determine the response according to the number of uncertainties. Among these methods, it is possible to refer to analyzes based on risk assessment, which are based on probabilistic methods and reliability. This chapter explains how to use probabilistic methods to describe uncertainty and assess risk as an analytical tool for decision making.

Sources of uncertainty in geotechnical engineering

Soil and rock are non-homogeneous and non-homogeneous environments that are generally defined by a number of geometrical, mechanical and resistance parameters. These parameters may show different values in two different points of the same environment. Therefore, it is not possible to specify their values at any point except by precise measurement.

Selection of soil geotechnical parameters has always been one of the most challenging problems for engineers due to the uncertainties in this field. These parameters cannot be precisely determined due to existing uncertainties. Uncertainties in geotechnical engineering can generally be divided into two general categories: Inherent uncertainties and cognitive uncertainties (Griffiths and Fenton, 2007).

Inherent soil uncertainties are caused by the random nature of soil parameters at different points and times. Each layer of soil has been affected by various factors such as physical, chemical and geological changes over time and have caused changes in the soil. These uncertainties are related to some parameters of the environment and the studied system or some phenomena that are going to occur, such as the level of underground water, the amount of adhesion, the angle of internal friction, the magnitude of the earthquake, the return period of the phenomena and other things. According to the nature of this category of sources of uncertainty, it is not possible to reduce or eliminate these uncertainties and it should be properly considered in the process of geotechnical designs (Phoon, 2008)).

Cognitive uncertainty is caused by the lack of information about a parameter. Cognitive uncertainties include uncertainty in measuring parameters (such as measuring SPT, CPT and similar cases), statistical uncertainties (caused by limited information) and uncertainty of conventional models. Uncertainties caused by the transformation of laboratory data into design parameters can also be included in this group.

Uncertainty in the measurement of geotechnical parameters is affected by the accuracy of the device and the user. The accuracy of the device is generally determined by the manufacturing companies. Economic considerations in the study stages of geotechnical structures always lead to a reduction in the number of boreholes and statistical uncertainties.

The uncertainty of the model is defined as the ratio of the actual value to the value predicted by the model. Uncertainties of the model are caused by the idealizations done in solving the physical equations. According to the above explanations, it can be said that the cognitive uncertainties can be reduced to some extent by increasing the accuracy and the number of samples.

Some researchers classify geotechnical engineering uncertainty sources into two categories, parametric uncertainties and model uncertainties. In this classification, all error sources that lead to uncertainty in geotechnical characteristics are classified as parametric uncertainty and errors caused by conventional models are classified as model uncertainties.

Considering the uncertainties in the determination of geotechnical parameters, the use of deterministic analysis using deterministic parameters does not seem very logical. Using statistical variable parameters is the best way to express these parameters. The uncertainty of the variable X can be considered dependent on the standard deviation of the distribution of X, meaning that the effect of the uncertainties in the input parameters can be investigated with probabilistic models according to the standard deviation.

In order to analyze the stability of gables, it is necessary to determine the uncertainty in the input parameters. These uncertainties are expressed by probability distribution functions and probability components (mean value and standard deviation).

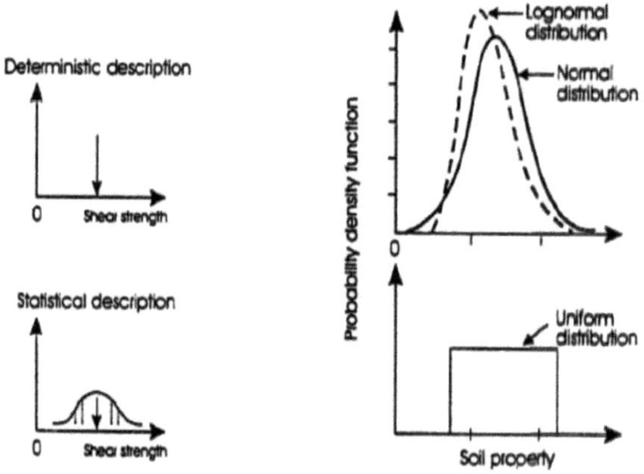

Figure 9. Comparison of definition of variable parameters by deterministic and probabilistic method

Therefore, with the help of mean parameters, standard deviation and probability distribution function, the variable parameter can be defined simply, while using the coefficient of variation instead of the standard deviation is more useful. Figure (9a) shows the expression of geotechnical parameters in definite and probabilistic form. Figure (9b) shows probability distribution functions commonly used in geotechnical engineering. Common probability distribution functions in geotechnical engineering are normal distribution, log normal and uniform distribution. These functions are very simple and understandable.

In traditional analysis, design adequacy is expressed by confidence factor. There is no clear relationship between the confidence coefficient and the probability of breakage. In other words, a slope with a higher confidence coefficient may have less stability than a slope with a lower confidence coefficient. For example, a confidence coefficient of 1.5 with a standard deviation of 0.5 can have a very high probability of breakage. more than the confidence coefficient of 1.2 with a standard deviation of 0.1. Therefore, the uncertainties in geotechnical engineering and the ineffectiveness of the conventional methods show the necessity of using risk-based methods. In the following, we will explain the principles and basics of risk-based methods.

Estimation of average and standard deviation of geotechnical parameters

One of the basic arts of geotechnical engineering science is the ability to logically estimate the values of problem parameters with limited data and information about that parameter. Appropriate estimation of soil mechanical properties for different purposes is usually expressed by two numbers:

- ❖ The best estimate and;
- ❖ The amount of uncertainty expressed by the concepts of mean value and standard deviation, respectively.

In order to perform the reliability analysis and calculate the probability of occurrence, it is necessary to estimate the mean and standard deviation of all the parameters involved in the problem.

The best estimate

The best estimate of geotechnical parameters is the average value, which is determined from the following equation.

$$m_x = \frac{1}{n}\sum x_i$$

In this relationship, x_i is the random data values, n is the number of data and m_x is the average of the data.

Uncertainty

The amount of data dispersion around the real value in a statistical distribution is defined by a quantity known as the standard deviation. If the standard deviation has a large value, it indicates the high dispersion of the distribution, and if it is zero, it indicates that all the measurements are equal to the average value, in which case it is said that the uncertainty of the measurements is zero. Based on the amount of data available, there are various methods to estimate the standard deviation. It is more common to use 3 methods in geotechnical problems, which are described below (Duncan, 2000).

Calculation of standard deviation based on available data

To calculate the value of the standard deviation, if sufficient data is available, the following basic relationship can be used.

$$\sigma = \sqrt{\frac{\sum (X_i - \bar{X})^2}{N-1}}$$

So that in this relationship, X_i is the i-th value of X, $\bar{X}$ the average of the values of X and N is the total number of data.

The use of equation 2-3 to calculate the standard deviation creates many limitations for assessing reliability in geotechnical engineering problems. Because in most geotechnical problems, there is not enough data to use this relationship. In order to apply the methods of reliability analysis in such problems, i.e. in situations where there is not enough data to use the equation, one should look for other methods to calculate the standard deviation. In the following, two other methods for calculating the standard deviation, which are more common in solving geotechnical problems, are described.

Calculation of standard deviation using the coefficient of variation

One of the methods of estimating the value of the standard deviation, when sufficient data is not available to use the equation below, is the use of published values, which are usually expressed in terms of the coefficient of variation.

$$COV = \frac{S\tan dard\,Deviation}{Mean} = \frac{\sigma}{\bar{x}}$$

In this regard, COV is the coefficient of variation. Using the above relationship and knowing the average and coefficient of variation of the investigated geotechnical parameter, the value of the standard deviation can be calculated as follows:

$$\sigma = COV.\bar{X}$$

The coefficient of variation values for a number of geotechnical parameters and local tests are given in table 1.

Table 1. Values of coefficient of variation of geotechnical characteristics

Property or In-Situ Test Result	COV (%)	Source
Unit Weight (γ)	3-20	Phoon et al (1995)
Friction Angle (ϕ)	7-12	Harr (1987)
Cohesion (c)	40	Harr (1987)
Compression index (Cc)	10-37	Harr (1984), Kulhawy (1993),
Standard Penetration Test (N)	10-45	Harr (1984), Kulhawy (1993)
Electric cone penetration test (qc)	5-15	Kulhawy (1993)
Mechanical cone penetration test (qc)	15-37	Harr (1984), Kulhawy (1993)
Undrained Shear Strength (S_u)	5-15	Lacasse and Nadim (1997), Duncan (2000)

The use of the values in this table results in a general and approximate estimate of the standard deviation of the studied parameters, which requires the use of engineering judgment and accounting for the uncertainties caused by the use of these values.

Calculation of standard deviation based on the law of three standard deviations

This empirical rule was presented by Ho and Wang (1992). The presentation of this rule is based on the fact that by considering 3 standard deviations on the sides of the average parameter with a normal distribution, 99.37% of the possible values for that parameter are covered. Therefore, if HCV is the highest possible value for the normal parameter under investigation and LCV is the lowest possible value for the normal parameter under investigation, these values can be approximately equal to 3 standard deviations above and 3 standard deviations below the average value, respectively. Therefore, with a reasonable initial estimate of the maximum and minimum possible values for each parameter with the normal distribution function and using the equation, the value of the standard deviation can be determined.

$$\sigma = \frac{HCV - LCV}{6}$$

Risk and safety

The process of identifying what things will happen, when and why, and what consequences they will have if they do happen is called risk identification. Accepting the consequences of an event is called risk taking. Risk exists in all projects and must be identified. Steps must be taken to strike a balance between economy and safety. In excavations to calculate risk, firstly, we must use the knowledge and guidance of experts and experienced people to be able to estimate the range of solutions, secondly, we must decide the safety range or the degree of risk in economic considerations and factors, and the amount that will result from rupture determine what we lose. In calculating the risk, the economic differences and the performance of the temporary and permanent structure should also be considered.

In topic 12 of the National Building Regulations, a temporary structure is a structure that is temporarily implemented to equip the workshop and to carry out main and protective operations. The word "Temporary" usually causes mistakes. In many works, measuring the strength and durability of soil stabilizers and controlling underground water requires sufficient resistance and durability for many years, especially in deep and wide excavations in big cities, where the pit lasts for a long time. In this case, the designer of the temporary structure has the duty to provide a sufficient and reliable solution, but in accordance with the time and without wasting materials and imposing unpredictable costs.

Therefore, in the design of many excavation programs, the probability of rupture or deformation due to the risk related to the safety and life of others should be very low. Decision-making and decision-making based on existing risks are done when the loss of the economy is considered and not the loss or jeopardy of people's safety and health. Therefore, in the design of many dredging programs, the risk should be carefully identified first (Puller, 2003).

In risk assessment, the calculation of initial costs, construction costs, costs due to breakage and probability of breakage are determined in relation to different stabilization methods. Table (2-3) shows the risk and safety factors suggested for overall stability. As can be seen in the table, the safety factor is determined according to life risk and economic risk, and with the increase of economic risk and life risk, the safety factor increases, and as a result, stabilization costs also increase.

Table 2. Suggested safety factor for overall stability (Shaw-Shong, 2005)

life risk			Economic risk
Much	Low	Insignificant	
1.4	1.2	>۱	Insignificant
1.4	1.2	1.2	Low
1.4	1.4	1.4	Much

The above safety coefficients can be modified according to the conditions of Iran, especially in terms of the impact of human errors in the stages of studies and implementation and the lack of implementation of the quality control system in all executive departments.

Excavation safety issues can be divided into the following three main categories:
- Safety of employees in and around the pit and passersby and vehicles against possible accidents, especially the risk of the pit falling.
- The risk of damage and destruction of buildings adjacent to the pit due to excavation or collapse of the pit.
- The risk of damage to urban facilities and arteries due to excavation or collapse of the pit.

Methods based on risk assessment

Researchers have always sought to quantify phenomena and use probabilistic theories to model and analyze them. The quantification of phenomena and the use of probability theories were considered in the 16th and 17th centuries. The issue of risk and its management was also raised a few years after that and it quickly received attention in various sciences, but its current form was raised after 1960, which led to the emergence of insurance. Due to the introduction of geotechnical uncertainties in the last few years, risk management quickly entered this discussion so that it has become one of the important parts of this science.

The analysis of geotechnical structures based on risk assessment is a topic that has recently attracted the attention of researchers. The reason for this approach is the existence of non-deterministic parameters or uncertainties in geotechnical issues. Because the existence of uncertainties leads to unsafe designs. Therefore, the degree of design uncertainty and the risks caused by this design should be evaluated in order to reduce the number of damages by risk management.

As mentioned, geotechnical engineers consider the capacity of the plan more than the required amount of the project due to the existence of uncertainties. The ratio of capacity to demand (reliability factor) is usually chosen based on experience. This method has some problems, one of which is the conservativeness of this method. The design based on risk assessment can cover some of the limitations of the certainty factor. Design based on risk assessment means trying to quantify the inherent uncertainties of an engineering problem and how to deal with them.

Advantages of risk assessment

Conducting a risk assessment will bring the following benefits:

- ➢ Clear and clear solutions about existing uncertainties;
- ➢ Providing a logical and systematic process;
- ➢ Comprehensive evaluation about safety;
- ➢ Providing reasonable and usually quantitative bases for comparing existing risks;
- ➢ Providing a framework for optimal planning in order to reduce risk.

The role of risk assessment

The three important roles of risk assessment are:

- ❖ An auxiliary tool in traditional approaches;
- ❖ Alternative methods of traditional approaches;
- ❖ Basis for decision making.

Currently, despite the progress made in the approaches based on risk assessment, this method still does not replace the definitive and accepted existing methods, but instead of the conventional qualitative expressions such as "Safe" and "Unsafe", it deals with the numerical expression of the risk in a system.

Design based on risk and probability of failure

Risk means an event that occurs with a certain probability, and risk management includes planning and directing such events. An important part of the process of designing and operating geotechnical structures is risk management. Currently, this branch includes certain topics, titles and sub-sets which are schematically shown in figure (10).

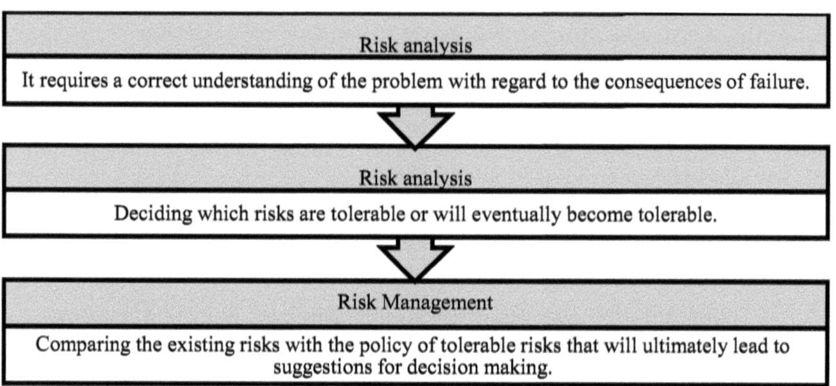

Figure 10. Quantitative risk assessment (Fell and Hartford, 1997)

In designs, the balance between safety and construction cost should be considered. It is possible to have an accurate design only if we have an accurate prediction of its performance, but since in reality such prediction accuracy is not accessible, as a result, using risk-based methods, economic benefits can be expressed as the basis for design. because this method enables at least the optimization of the part of the design that is related to uncertainties.

Optimal design is based on maintaining a balance between risk and cost. Probabilistic and statistical methods provide an effective tool for describing the lack of knowledge in models and input information and their coverage. Probability evaluation is much more effective than deterministic methods that only rely on the confidence factor. Because in infrastructures that have a low possibility of damage, the reliability coefficient cannot describe the conditions well, in other words, in structures that have a lot of damage consequences, reliability evaluation becomes more important.

The important point regarding the uncertainty in the reliability coefficient is the existence of chance. If the analysis is correct and the parameters are chosen correctly, then the reliability coefficient is a judgment criterion. The chance factor can be named as the probability of failure, which is obtained from the following relationship.

$$P_f = P\{F.S < 1\}$$

However, an increase in conservatism leads to a decrease in the probability of improper performance of the structure. At the same time, it increases the cost of construction. A degree of conservatism where an increase in construction cost results in a significant reduction in risk can be cost-effective. Recently, studies have been conducted with the aim of improving risk factors, emphasizing the importance of uncertainty analysis and validating probabilistic methods as a useful tool for decision making. One of the important features in risk assessment is that subsequent decisions are facilitated by analyzing different risk modes (for example, cost-benefit analysis).

Calculating the probability of failure using reliability analysis

In recent years, according to the sources of uncertainty in the field of geotechnical engineering, probabilistic analysis and reliability assessment have been given a lot of attention due to economic and safety issues in civil engineering. In the design and analysis related to geotechnical engineering, decisions are mainly dependent on the response of the system under the design conditions.

If some components of a system are uncertain, the response of this system cannot be evaluated with sufficient certainty and accuracy. In fact, due to the existence of uncertainties, the design in the old and common way, i.e. deterministic design, is under question due to their inability to account for system response errors and in fact output uncertainties. While in the design and analysis, considering the uncertainties, evaluating and checking the statistical characteristics of the outputs of a system as a function of uncertain parameters are effective in it.

In designs and simulations related to geotechnical engineering, design parameters and system outputs are a function of many parameters, most of which cannot be determined accurately and correctly. The task of uncertainty analysis is to determine system output uncertainties as a function of model uncertainties and parameters affecting the system. This method of analysis actually provides a specific and systematic framework to quantify the uncertainty of the system output. In addition, this analysis helps the designer to find a suitable view of the contribution of each of the uncertain parameters in the overall uncertainty of the system output. Reliability analysis includes a set of methods that manage ambiguities and uncertainties using the break probability or probability distribution of the basis function.

In fact, reliability analysis methods transfer the uncertainties of the input parameters to the output values of the function, or in other words, the effect of the uncertainties of the input parameters will be applied to the output values. This method has two advantages, firstly, the uncertainties are managed in a logical way in the design and calculations, and the sensitivity of the different design variables is accurately analyzed or determined. Second, these methods have a more logical basis than the decision-making of completely deterministic analyzes (Beacher and Christian, 2003).

Reliability analysis methods are generally divided into three categories: Analytical methods, approximate methods, and simulation methods. In analytical methods, the probability density function of the input parameters is mathematically expressed and then the reliability coefficient relationship is integrated based on the input variable parameters. By doing this, the probability density function of the confidence coefficient is determined. Fewer studies have been done in this method due to the mathematical complexity. The method of compound random variable curve (JDRV) is one of the mathematical methods used to analyze reliability (Johari, 2013).

Approximate methods of reliability analysis calculate the probability of occurrence of the phenomenon by using probability indicators such as mean, standard deviation and coefficient of variation. In approximate methods to estimate the probability of occurrence and evaluate the reliability of the performance function at the closest point to the target point. In recent years, approximate methods have attracted the attention of many researchers and a lot of research has been done in this field. Common approximation methods are the first-second-order moment method (FOSM), the advanced second-order first-order moment method (AFOSM), and the point estimation method (PEM). Of course, the advanced second-order torque method is also performed in other ways, and each one has different details.

The collection of these methods is known as first-order reliability analysis (FORM) method (Juang et al., 2004). Each of these methods calculates the probability of failure with simplifying assumptions, and because of these simplifying assumptions, their accuracy has been reduced, and that is why these methods are called approximate methods. Approximate methods are able to estimate the mean and variance of the confidence coefficient, but are unable to provide any information about the shape of the probability density function. Therefore, the probability of occurrence of the phenomenon is obtained only by assuming the possible parametric distribution of the confidence coefficient (usually in normal or log-normal form). Approximate methods are also not accurate in modeling problems with a high degree of non-linearity.

Simulation methods are the most accurate methods of reliability analysis. In this method, it calculates the probability of occurrence of the phenomenon by simulating the random numbers of the input parameters and using repeated calculations. Today, with the development and expansion of computer hardware, the use of this method has also expanded. These methods are based on creating a set of answers that can be used to estimate the probability of occurrence. One of the techniques of this method is the Monte Carlo simulation method (MCS), which is the creation of numerical values of basic variables to solve the structural problem of mixed random variables.

A large number of simulations are needed to get closer to reality and the desired approximation, but fortunately for practical problems, the results will converge after a few thousand repetitions. In cases where numerical methods are used, methods have been proposed to reduce the number of repetitions required (Rajabalinejad, 2009).

Considering the importance and application of the mentioned methods, the principles and basics of some conventional methods have been discussed in the following.

The method of combining the distribution curve of random variables

The curve combination method of random variables (JDRV) is an analytical probabilistic method. In this method, a probability distribution function with a specific mathematical relationship is considered for each of the input variables. Then, using the relations governing the method of combining the distribution curve of variables and according to the arrangement of different parameters in the performance function, the probability distribution function of the input variables is combined with each other and finally the probability distribution curve of the performance function is obtained (Johari, 2013).

Point estimation method (PEM)

The point estimation method is one of the simplest reliability approximation methods that calculates the mean and variance of the performance function by approximating the points. This method was first presented by Rosenbluth (1975). He has considered three general modes for this method:

- ❖ If Y is a function of variable X with mean, standard deviation and skewness.
- ❖ If Y is a function of variable X with symmetrical and almost normal distribution.
- ❖ If Y is a function of n variables X_1, X_2, X_3, ..., X_n with symmetric distribution, such that these variables are independent or correlated.

First order second anchor method (FOSM)

This method is a relatively simple method for calculating the effect of changes in random input data according to the performance function. In this function, the performance function is the relationship of the confidence coefficient in the limit equilibrium method, such as the simplified Bishop method, Morgenstern-Price and Spencer method. (Harr 1987).

The application of the FOSM method in slope stability analysis by researchers such as Alonso (1976), Tang et al. (1976, Wenmark (b1977), Lee and Lamb (1987), Lee and Witt (1987), Mustin and Suo (1992), Christian et al. (1994), and Duncan (2000) and many others have been reviewed. Although the FOSM method is relatively simple, it also has some limitations. The accuracy of the FOSM method is low due to the non-linearity of the Taylor series fitting in the performance function. It should be noted that the reliability coefficient equations for most limit equilibrium methods are non-linear. In addition, the FOSM method does not output any information about the shape of the probability density function (PDF), and the shape (PDF) must be assumed to approximate any probability (El-Ramly et al. 2002, Griffiths et al. 2002b). The first-order second anchor method is an approximate method for estimating the mean value and standard deviation of functions such as Y, which have one or more random variables. In general, to calculate the mean and standard deviation of the function Y, the probability distribution function of the random variables that make up this function is needed, while in many practical problems, the available information about the random variables is limited only to their mean and standard deviation. (Ang and Tang, 1984). This method only considers the average and the coefficient of variation of the performance function (for example, the reliability coefficient) and is not able to consider the coefficient of variation of the input parameters.

If Y is a function consisting of n random variables x_1, x_2, ..., x_n, we have:

$$Y = f(x_1, x_2, ..., x_n)$$

In this method, the approximate value of the mean and standard deviation of the Y function is performed by using the Taylor series of the function around the mean value of the random variables and regardless of the higher order terms. In the case that the expansion of the Taylor series has only linear terms and higher order terms are omitted, the first order estimate of the mean and the second order moment equals the standard deviation:

$$\mu_y \approx f(\mu_{x1}, \mu_{x2}, ..., \mu_{xn})$$

$$\sigma_y^2 \approx \{b\}^T [C]\{b\}$$

So that the vector represents the estimated values for at points xi, in other words:

$$\{b\}^T = \{\partial Y / \partial x1, \partial Y / \partial x2, ..., \partial Y / \partial xn\}_{\mu i}$$

The matrix [C] is the covariance matrix and is equal to:

$$[C] = [\sigma][R][\sigma]$$

$[\sigma]$ in this regard, a diagonal matrix is a standard deviation and R is a correlation matrix with diagonal members $R_{ii} = 1$ and $R_{ij} = P_{ij}$ non-diagonal members (where P_{ij} is the $C_{ij} = \sigma_i \sigma_j R_{ij}$ correlation coefficient between random variable i and j). The scalar form of the matrix [C] is as follows:

$$\sigma_Y^2 \approx \sum_{i=1}^{n} \left(\frac{\partial Y}{\partial x_i} \right) \cdot \sigma_{x_i}^2$$

If there is no correlation between the variables $(\rho_{ij} = 0)$.

Advanced first-order second moment method (AFOSM)

This method is defined by Hasofcr and Lind (1974) and is usually known by the same name, where all the relationships used are similar to the FOSM method. Based on this, the results of this method are similar to the FOSM method. In this method, the reliability index of the second moment (β) takes into account the effect of both parameters, the average value and the coefficient of variation of random parameters effective in the design, and also evaluates the effect of the type and distribution of random probabilities. In this method, it is usually assumed that the safety function has a normal distribution and the β index represents the average distance of the safety function from the critical value in standard deviation units, as follows:

$$\beta = \frac{\mu_f - C_f}{\sigma_f}$$

In this regard, μ_f the average value of the safety function, C_f is the critical value and σ_f is the standard deviation. For example, for the system stability problem with driving force Q and resistance R, with the governing equation M=Q-R, where both variables Q and R have a normal distribution function, the value of β is shown in figure (11). It should be noted that the critical value of M in this problem is equal to zero.

The first step in this method is to rewrite the relations of the investigated problem in terms of dimensionless variables. Each variable is identified by its corresponding i index. Each variable X_i is introduced with two indices, mean and standard deviation. By using the following relationship, all the variables of the problem are converted to unit less variables:

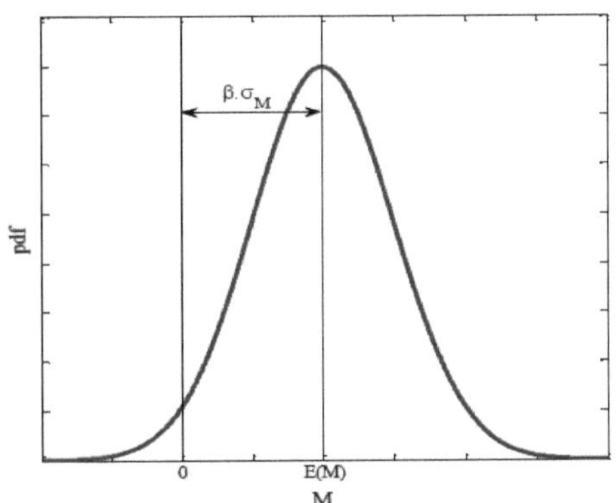

Figure 11. Display of β parameter and probability distribution function

$$x' = \frac{x_i - \mu_{xi}}{\sigma_{xi}}$$

That's mean:

$$x_i = \sigma_{xi} x_i' + \mu_{x_i}$$

By placing the value of random variables in terms of its equivalent dimensionless random variable from equation below in each performance function, the equivalent g function is obtained as a function of dimensionless variables:

$$g(x_1', x_2', \dots x_n') = 0$$

By deriving the above relation once, we have:

$$\frac{dx_i}{dx_i'} = \sigma_{xi}$$

Also, for function f we have:

$$\frac{\partial f}{\partial x_i'} = \frac{\partial f}{\partial x_i}\frac{dx_i}{dx_i'} = \sigma_{x_i}\frac{\partial f}{\partial x_i}$$

The gradient of the performance function (g) is defined as follows based on the Lagrangian method:

$$G = (\frac{\partial g}{\partial x_1'}, \frac{\partial g}{\partial x_2'}, ..., \frac{\partial g}{\partial x_n'})$$

By uniting the gradient vector G, the α vector is obtained as follows:

$$\alpha = \frac{G}{(G^T G)^{1/2}} \rightarrow \alpha_i = \frac{\left(\dfrac{\partial g}{\partial x_i'}\right)}{\sqrt{\displaystyle\sum_{i=1}^{n}\left(\dfrac{\partial g}{\partial x_i'}\right)}}$$

The calculation of the β index is done using the AFOSM method in 6 steps, which is called the Rakwitz iteration algorithm (Ang and Tang, 1984).

➢ Assuming an initial value for x_i^* :

$$x_i^* = \mu_{x_i}$$

Which is μ_{x_i} the average of the problem variables in the above relation.

➢ Calculation of G and α vectors in x_i^*

➢ Calculate new values for using the following relationship:

➢

$$x_i^* = \mu_{x_i} - \alpha_i \sigma_{x_i}$$

➤ Forming $g(x_1^*, x_2^*, ..., x_i^*) = 0$ and solving it for β.

➤ Calculation $x_i^* = -\alpha_i \beta$ using the value obtained from step 4.

➤ Repeat steps 1 to 5 until the cycle converges.

Low and Tang (1997) presented the following relationship to calculate the reliability index (β):

$$\beta = \min_{x \in F} \sqrt{\left[\frac{x_i - \mu_i}{\sigma_i}\right]^T [R]^{-1} \left[\frac{x_i - \mu_i}{\sigma_i}\right]}$$

where X_i is the representative vector of the set of random variables, μ_i is the average value, σ_i is the standard deviation, R is the correlation vector and F is the rupture area. The process of calculating the β index using the above relationship is as follows:

1. Calculation of μ and σ vectors and R matrices.
2. Calculate the value of β using equation 3-26.
3. Calculation of the minimum value of β by changing the values of the components of the X vector and observing the discontinuity criterion M=0.

Assuming the normal distribution of the safety function, by calculating the value of β, the probability of rupture can also be calculated as follows:

$$P_f = P[M \leq 0] = 1 - \phi(\beta) = \phi(-\beta)$$

Which ϕ is the standard normal cumulative distribution function.

As mentioned, the second-order first moment method also exists in other ways, and the collection of these methods is known as the first-order reliability analysis (FORM) method (Juang et al., 2004). In general, most of the approximate methods have been developed based on FORM and PEM methods.

Monte Carlo simulation method

One of the methods of determining the reliability indices is the Monte Carlo simulation method. This method is widely used in engineering. The Monte Carlo method is a computational algorithm that uses repeated random sampling to calculate results. The Monte Carlo method is usually used to simulate physical and mathematical systems using computers.

The Monte Carlo method is often used to solve mathematical problems with a large number of variables that are difficult to solve using analytical methods or other numerical methods. And in estimating probabilities and other indicators, the method of counting the number of occurrences is used. It should be mentioned that Monte Carlo simulation is actually related to a process in which the occurrence of states is random in all its aspects.

In general, the term Monte Carlo simulation or Monte Carlo method may be used to describe any technique that approximates the solution of quantitative problems through random sampling. But in this thesis, specifically, the term Monte Carlo simulation is used to describe a numerical method to determine the uncertainty in the output variables of the model by using the uncertainty in the input parameters. This method is a kind of simulation that clearly and quantitatively shows the uncertainty in different dimensions of the problem. In the Monte Carlo method, a probability distribution function is considered for each of the input random variables to quantify model uncertainties. If the input variables of the model are described as non-deterministic, the outputs of the model will necessarily be non-deterministic and will not end in a single solution. Therefore, the output of any method that uses the concept of probability distribution function for input variables for analysis will be a probability distribution function for the performance function. In order to determine the probability distribution of system performance, it is necessary to determine the uncertainty in the output of the system using the uncertainty in the input variables of the system, in other words, the uncertainty in the input variables should be transferred to the uncertainty in the results of the system.

There are different methods to determine (transfer) the uncertainty in the output variables of the system by using the uncertainties in the input parameters of the system. The Monte Carlo method is one of the simplest and most efficient of these methods. The Monte Carlo method effectively simulates the response of the performance function of the confidence coefficient to the input variables that are randomly selected and replaced in the performance function. In this method, random numbers are generated for each random input parameter according to the shape of its probability density function and its range of changes.

The generated random numbers are placed in the performance function and this process continues until the density function of the reliability coefficient is approximately determined and according to that the probability of breakage and the reliability index are calculated. Although the probability density function of each input random variable may have any shape, normal, log-normal, triangular and beta distributions are more common. Monte Carlo simulation has four stages (Hammond et al. 1991; Chandler, 1996):

❖ For each of the input random variables, a random value is selected according to its probability density function.

❖ The reliability coefficient value is calculated using the performance function and according to the numerical value selected in the first step.

❖ Steps one and two are repeated a large number of times and the value of the confidence factor is calculated for each repetition.

❖ Using the reliability coefficient values obtained from the previous steps, the probability of occurrence of unfavorable conditions P(F<FC), the mean value, the variance of the reliability coefficient and the shape of the probability density function of the reliability coefficient can be obtained.

It should be noted that Monte Carlo simulation uses different sequences of random numbers (a large number of computational steps). Therefore, it is possible that the probability of occurrence of inappropriate conditions, the average value, the variance and the shape of the probability density function are different in different sequences. If the calculation steps increase, these differences will decrease. The process of repeating the Monte Carlo cycle is carried out until we obtain a sufficient number of output variables to construct the probability distribution curve of the performance function. By repeating this operation many times, a large number of separate and independent values for the performance function are obtained. The number of repetitions required in the Monte Carlo method to construct the probability distribution function of the performance function depends on the level of safety, the desired accuracy for solving the problem, and the number of random variables involved in the problem. The number of iterations required for problems with input random variables can be approximated by the following equation: (Harr, 1987)

$$N = \left(\frac{d^2}{4(1-\varepsilon)^2} \right)^m$$

In this regard, N is the number of computational steps of Monte Carlo simulation, d and ε are respectively the normal standard deviation and the desired confidence level according to what is mentioned in table (3) and m is the number of input random variables.

Table 3. Standard deviations according to confidence levels (Abramson. 2002)

Confidence level	Standard deviation (d)
80%	1.282
90%	1.645
95%	1.960
99%	2.576

As can be seen from the above equation, the number of Monte Carlo iterations depends on the number of variables and the desired confidence level. For example, if the desired confidence level is 80%, then the standard deviation will be 1.28, and for a problem with one variable, 10 repetitions will be needed, and for a problem with two variables, 100 repetitions will be required. But if the desired confidence level is 90%, then the normal standard deviation will be 1.64, which requires 67 repetitions for a problem with one variable, 4489 for a problem with two variables, and 300,764 repetitions for a problem with 3 variables.

In fact, an infinite number of iterations would be required for the desired 100% confidence level. It is suggested that in order to avoid a large number of repetitions, according to the logical reasons, unnecessary random variables are not included in the calculation and the desired level of confidence is carefully selected. In practical cases, the number of Monte Carlo iterations is several thousand iterations, which may not be enough for very high confidence levels with a large number of variables. Fortunately, in most cases, after applying a few thousand repetitions, the problems will no longer be very sensitive to more repetitions. When the minimum number of calculation steps is determined, for each of the input random parameters, random numerical values are created and the confidence coefficient is determined using the performance function and according to the values created in each calculation problem.

To create random numbers, functions are often used that generate random numbers R_1, R_2, ..., R_n between zero and one and uniform probability distribution. Then, using the following relations, these numbers are converted into numbers with a standard normal probability distribution ($\mu = 0$, $\sigma = 1$) (Box and Muller, 1958).

$$N_1 = \sqrt{-2\ln R_1}\ \cos(2\pi R_2)$$

$$N_2 = \sqrt{-2\ln R_1}\ \sin(2\pi R_2)$$

R_1 and R_2 are random numbers generated with uniform distribution and N_2 and N_1 are independent random numbers with standard normal distribution. This process is continuously repeated until the required number of random numbers is generated, and finally the generated random numbers have mean $0=\mu$ and standard deviation $1=\sigma$. Equation below is used to convert numbers with standard normal distribution N_i to numbers with normal probability distribution with mean μ_x and standard deviation σ_x:

$$X_i = \mu_x + N_i\,\sigma_x$$

In this regard, X_i will be a random number with a normal distribution used in calculations related to the performance function and N_i will be a random number with a standard normal distribution.

The relationships presented are for the case where the generated random numbers are independent of each other. If random numbers with normal distribution are not independent of each other, then the second component of random numbers is calculated from the following equation:

$$N_2^* = N_1 \rho_{xy} + N_2 \sqrt{\left(1 - \rho^2_{xy}\right)}$$

In the above relationship, ρ_{xy} is the correlation coefficient between the random parameters X, Y and N_1, the first random number generated with a standard normal distribution, N_2 is the second random number with a standard normal distribution, and N_2 is a random number dependent on the number N_1. To generate interdependent random numbers with normal probability distribution, the following relationships can be used after generating random numbers:

$$X_1 = \mu_x + N_1 \sigma_x$$

$$Y_1 = \mu_y + N_2^* \sigma_x$$

After generating random numbers with the required characteristics, the reliability coefficient for each group of numbers is calculated using the performance function. With the reliability coefficient values obtained from the simulation, the probability of improper performance can be calculated from the following relationship (Abramson, 2002):

$$P(F < F_c) = \frac{n_c}{n_{total}}$$

In this regard, n_c is the number of simulation repetitions in which the confidence factor is less than F_c and n_{total} is the total number of Monte Carlo simulation steps. The final result of the Monte Carlo simulation can be shown in the form of a histogram and the values of the probability of occurrence and the reliability index can be calculated.

Summary

In all subjects related to engineering sciences, there are uncertainties that must be properly considered to obtain acceptable results. Despite these uncertainties in a system, the behavior of this system cannot be reliably evaluated during design and analysis. In traditional methods, due to the existence of these uncertainties, the capacity of the plan is considered more than the required amount of the project. These methods are very conservative and a clear relationship between the reliability coefficient and the probability of failure is not defined in them.

But if the analysis and design is done by considering the uncertainties in the system, the evaluation and checking of the statistical characteristics of the outputs of a system is expressed as a function of the uncertain parameters effective in it. Design based on risk assessment as an auxiliary tool for quantifying uncertainties covers some of the limitations of the certainty factor. This means that the impact of the uncertainty of the input parameters will be applied to the output values. This method has two advantages, firstly, the uncertainties are managed in a logical way in the design and calculations, and the sensitivity of different design variables is accurately analyzed or determined. Second, these methods have a more logical basis than the decision-making of completely deterministic analyses.

The effectiveness of using risk assessment techniques in engineering problems has been proven due to making it possible to investigate damage mechanisms more accurately than deterministic methods. On the other hand, the probability of failure is less, the cost of risk is lower, so geotechnical engineers use the probability of failure as an effective factor in risk-based design. One of the results of risk-based design is to quantify the reliability of the structure in the form of reliability index. In order to be able to fully use the advantages of probabilistic analysis, it is necessary to use an advanced model and a suitable reliability technique. Reliability methods are generally divided into three categories: Analytical methods, approximate methods, and simulation methods. According to the materials mentioned in this chapter, it seems that the most accurate method of reliability analysis is the use of simulation methods. This method analyzes events by creating random numbers in the range of input parameters in cases where the mathematical solution of the equations is not possible. In recent years, with the advancement of hardware, the tendency to use simulation methods has also increased. Monte Carlo simulation method is one of the most suitable simulation methods. In this thesis, the reliability analysis of well stability using Monte Carlo simulation method is considered.

Chapter IV

Evaluation of Well Stability by Monte Carlo Simulation Method

Introduction

Many of the ruling theories in geotechnical engineering are based on the laws of mechanics of continuous environments. Earth materials do not follow the laws of continuous environments due to porosity and many uncertainties. Due to this issue, the use of semi-empirical methods based on field tests has been expanded. One of the key issues in the geotechnical analysis of structures is the selection of geotechnical parameters of soil materials.

The selection of soil parameters is always influenced by sources of uncertainty, which makes engineering judgment in this field very difficult. In recent years, geotechnical engineers have proposed risk assessment methods and probabilistic methods instead of deterministic analyzes in order to solve this problem. As stated in the previous chapter, these methods consider the amount of uncertainties quantitatively by creating a logical framework and carry out the design according to the amount of uncertainties. Probability methods and reliability analysis were examined in the third chapter, and as mentioned, the Monte Carlo simulation method is one of the precise methods in this field that has attracted the attention of researchers in recent years. In this chapter, the process of risk assessment is explained first, and then the effectiveness of using the Monte Carlo simulation method to evaluate the effect of parametric uncertainties in well stability analysis is discussed with an applied example solution.

Quantitative risk assessment process

In the international workshop in 1997, the latest achievements of quantitative landslide risk assessment were reviewed (Graden & Fell, 1997). In this workshop, the work of a group consisting of various international technical organizations and companies supported by the International Union of Geological Scientists (IUGS) expressed the results of their investigations. In 1996, a meeting was held in Trondheim with the presence of the IUGS working group consisting of the Landslide Risk Assessment Technical Committee chaired by Professor Robin Fell from the School of Civil Engineering, University of New South Wales, Australia. Until then, the use of risk analysis was limited to only a few countries, including Australia, Canada, South Africa, and the United States of America.

The goals of this group work were

> ➤ Reviewing technical terms and providing internationally accepted definitions used in landslide risk assessment.
> ➤ Reviewing international standards regarding accepted risks and providing methods of applying them in landslide risk.
> ➤ Reviewing the methods of predicting the vulnerability of characteristics and durability against landslides.

The main stages of risk assessment are:

> ➤ Risk analysis (estimation of risks);
> ➤ Risk assessment (deciding which risks are tolerable or will eventually be tolerable).
> ➤ Comparison of existing risks with the tolerable risks policy, which will ultimately lead to suggestions for decision making.

Simultaneous attention to the three stages of risk analysis and risk assessment along with risk control leads to risk management. Risk control also includes examining options for dealing with risk, such as reducing risk, accepting risk, or avoiding risk. Both risk analysis and risk management must meet the needs of challenging construction projects. Combining risk analysis with risk management leads to a successful project that meets expectations. Risk analysis and risk management are intertwined in a geotechnical risk management process. If each of the stages of risk assessment is well examined, the benefit from applying risk management will be noticeable.

Quantitative assessment of risk in Piedra pit

Traditional methods of slope stability assessment are based on empirical judgments such as the concept of confidence factor. Today, studies have been conducted on methods that can help geotechnical engineers in quantifying uncertainties effective in the stability of slopes. In this method, both traditional and numerical analytical methods are used to quantify the uncertainties or existing risks and it is presented in the form of a reference called Quantitative Risk Assessment (QRA).

Assessment of soil slope stability includes significant uncertainties. These uncertainties come from changes in soil, rock, and underground water conditions in the region. The engineering specifications represent the materials of the pits (parametric uncertainties section) and the uncertainty in how the pit works during stability (the model uncertainty section).

Quantitative risk assessment can be used in the concept of slope stability to find alternative methods and to recognize the engineering judgment process. Quantitative risk assessment includes two parts: Assessing the probability of slope failure and identifying the consequences of failure. Quantitative risk assessment can also be used to assess the risk of failure of excavations, embankments and retaining walls and lands subject to slope instability. Assessing the risk of excavations in the first place seems very difficult. Because the accurate estimation of most of the input parameters to quantify the risk is very difficult and expensive. As mentioned, the quantitative risk assessment method does not replace the definitive and accepted existing methods, but instead of the conventional qualitative expressions such as "Safe" and "Unsafe" expressions, it deals with the numerical expression of the risk in a system.

Risk acceptance and tolerability criteria

Specialists have provided different criteria for a level of risk that is tolerable or acceptable, but one of the most comprehensive categories is as follows (Fell & Hartford, 1997).

Widely acceptable risk: If the annual risk of losses is significantly less than, it is usually considered as a negligible risk.

Unacceptable risk: If the annual risk of casualties exceeds normal conditions, it is considered unacceptable.

Tolerable risk: If the annual risk of casualties is between, it is tolerable.

The tolerable levels of risk can be estimated using the ALARP principle. This principle deals with valuing and weighing risk against the amount of effort, time and money needed to control that risk. Therefore, ALARP specifies the level at which risk-related issues are expected to be under control.

Decision making based on risk

One of the most important challenges faced by the geotechnical engineer is the decision to choose soil resistance parameters used in engineering analysis. These decisions are based on information that is always somewhat uncertain. Therefore, the decision-making process includes two factors: Uncertainty in decision variables and project risk level. Several decision-making algorithms have been used in the history of geotechnical engineering, the most important of which are: The worst-case method, techniques based on reliability analysis, and the confidence interval method.

The goal of the worst case method is to obtain the complete safety of the project and pay attention to the most possible risks. For example, if the range of the friction angle measured for the sand deposit is in the range of 30-40 degrees, the design value is considered 30 degrees. This method is very conservative.

The reliability method relies on the selection of the design parameter to provide the desired degree of reliability or for a specific failure probability. For example, regarding soil design parameters, the value of reliability index is assumed to be three for normal slopes and four for critical slopes.

The main advantage of risk-based methods compared to deterministic methods is the possibility of using engineering judgment according to the acceptable level of risk for the problem under consideration in making decisions. One of the results of using risk-based methods and reliability analysis is calculating the probability of failure. Calculating the probability of failure makes it possible to make an appropriate engineering judgment according to the site conditions and the degree of importance of the structure. For example, it is clear that the design of a nuclear power plant site and a normal building are significantly different in terms of the degree of importance and the amount of damage caused by their failure.

In table (4) the performance index expected by the engineers of the US Army Ground Force for evaluating the slopes is presented, which can be used to make the appropriate decision based on the required performance of the structure and using this criterion.

Table 4. The expected performance index of the slopes based on the reliability index

Probability of failure	Reliability index (β)	Expected performance
0.16	1	Dangerous
0.07	1.5	Unsuitable
0.023	2	Bad
0.006	2.5	Less than average
0.001	3	More than average
0.00003	4	Good
0.0000003	5	Excellent

Also, in figure (12) the value of the probability of damage allowed for civil structures is specified. Of course, in order to be able to use these charts, it is necessary to obtain quantitative values by performing reliability analysis. According to the figure (12) provided by the engineers of the US Army, the reliability of the structure can be estimated to some extent by determining the reliability index in terms of failure mode.

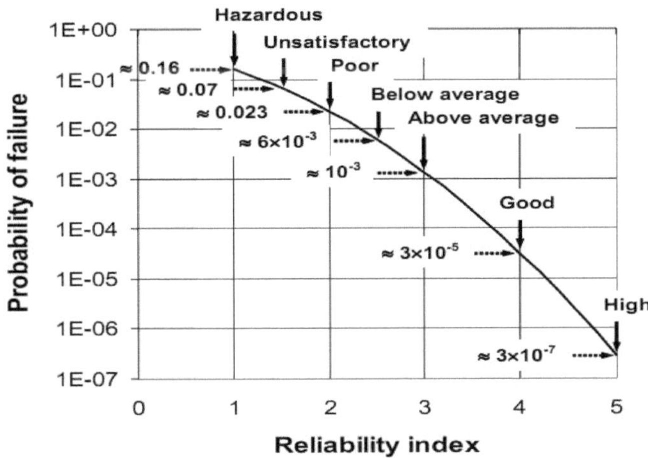

Figure 12. Permissible values of breakage probability and reliability index

In this method, soil parameters are introduced as ranges with a degree of certainty. Normally, design parameters are selected with 90% confidence level.

Risk management in excavation projects

Excavation risk management is a systematic process including the following:

> Identify risks;

> If necessary, assess the risk arising from these risks;

> Implementation of control measures;

> Checking the effectiveness of control measures.

Risk management process

Risk identification: The first step in the risk management process is to identify the risks caused by excavation. For example, risks such as:

> Underground facilities such as gas, electricity and sewage. (The exact location of underground facilities must be determined before excavation).

> Falling by falling soil or stone.

> Improper placement of materials inside the pit, equipment or other forces.

> Instability of structures near the pit.

- Any history of ground disturbance in previous excavations.
- The possibility of water or any other liquid settling into the pit.
- Dangerous vibrations.

Risk assessment

Risk assessment helps in deciding which control measures to implement. for example:

- Identifying who is at risk.
- Determining the source or process that causes risk.
- Identifying the control measures that should be taken.
- Checking the effectiveness of control measures.

In the risk assessment of dredging projects, these items should also be considered:

- Local conditions such as access, land slope, nearby buildings, underground water.
- Excavation depth.
- Soil characteristics such as shear strength, stability, layering, adhesion.
- Any need for a special program or work method.
- Number of people at risk.
- Weather conditions of the region.
- Excavation duration.

Risk control: Hierarchy of control measures: Some control measures are of special importance. Control measures can be graded from the highest level of protection and reliability to the lowest. This ranking is known as risk control hierarchy.

The most effective control is risk elimination, but if risk elimination is impractical, the risk should be reduced with one of the following methods:

- **Displacement:** for example, using a stone crusher instead of manual methods.

➢ **Separation:** Such as using a concrete wall to separate the sidewalk and mobile devices to reduce the risk of accidents.

➢ **Engineering measures:** Such as piling and creating berms on the sides of excavations to reduce the risk of landslides.

If the risk remains, it should be reduced through measures such as the installation of danger signs and the use of safety work clothes. The table below shows some risks in dredging projects and control measures.

Table 5. Examples of risk control measures

Potential risks	An example of control measures
Landslide Water leakage Falling Danger Underground facilities	Creating a berm or installing protection (such as piling) Use of pumping with other water collection systems Creating ramps, stairs or other suitable accesses into the pit Obtaining information from the authorities regarding underground facilities

Well stability evaluation by Monte Carlo simulation method

Considering the inherent variability of soil, risk-based methods and reliability analysis are preferable to deterministic analysis. As mentioned earlier, the Monte Carlo simulation method is the most accurate reliability analysis method. In this method, the probability of liquefaction is obtained directly from the simulation of the input parameters. Evaluation of well stability by Monte Carlo simulation method has four steps as follows:

❖ Random parameters are generated based on their mean, coefficient of variation and probability distribution function.

❖ The reliability coefficient value is calculated using the performance function and according to the numerical value selected in the first step.

* Steps one and two are repeated a large number of times and the reliability coefficient value is calculated for each repetition.

* The probability of liquefaction is equal to the level under the confidence factor diagram in the range of answers smaller than one. Figure (13) shows an example of failure probability calculation. The area under the graph is equal to the ratio of the number of responses smaller than one to the total number of repetitions.

$$P_f = \frac{N_f}{N_{total}}$$

In the above relationship, N_f is the number of responses smaller than one and N_{total} is the total number of repetitions.

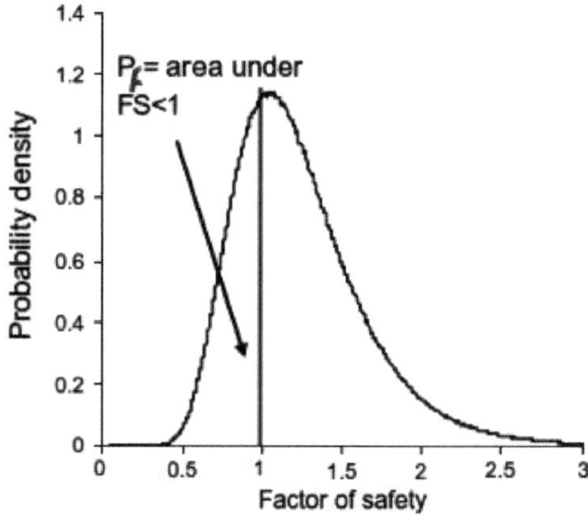

Figure 13. Probability density diagram of reliability coefficient and failure probability calculation

The first step in Monte Carlo simulation is generating input random numbers. Random numbers are made based on average parameters, coefficient of variation, hypothetical probability distribution function and correlation between parameters. As described in the third chapter, the change coefficient of soil parameters can be calculated in three ways. Due to existing limitations, the use of coefficients suggested by previous researchers is the most useful in reliability analysis. The specifications of the random parameters are considered according to table (6).

Table 6. Specifications of random parameters

Parameter	Probability density function	Coefficient of variation (%COV)
γ	Normal	7
C	Normal log	40
φ	Normal	10

Common probability distribution function in geotechnical parameters are: Normal distribution, log normal distribution and beta distribution. In the technical literature, the type of probability distribution function is proposed for the parameters whose coefficient of variation is less than 25%, normal distribution and if the coefficient of variation is more than 25%, log normal distribution. The log-normal probability distribution function with a coefficient of variation greater than 25% is very close to the normal state.

Solving a sample example

Among the pit stabilization methods mentioned in chapter II, the nailing method has significant relative advantages. This method is one of the most suitable methods for stabilizing the excavation wall in terms of execution speed, acceptable cost, quick and easy adaptation to the conditions of different sites, no need for heavy machinery, fast and reliable implementation of waterproofing, and no interference of the guard structure with the main operation of the building.

Considering that the nailing method has been used in recent years in Tehran and some other big cities of Iran to stabilize excavation walls, therefore, in this section, an attempt has been made to analyze the possibilities of this method. The software used in this thesis is SLOPE/W from the Geo Studio software collection. SLOPE/W is a software that calculates the safety factor of soil and stone slopes using the limit equilibrium method in different ways. This software includes a set of drawing methods for analysis. One of the most important capabilities of this program is the possibility of modeling common reinforcements such as harnesses, nailing's and geo fabrics in order to increase the safety of slopes.

Also, this software has the ability to analyze probabilities and provide an index of reliability and probability of failure. In order to perform the analysis and obtain the reliability index and the probability of breakage in the nailed walls, it is necessary to consider a specific model. Despite the variety of available reports for the design of structures such as buildings, dams and bridges, due to the newness of nailing compared to other technologies, separate national and international reports have not been prepared and presented for it. But most designers refer to the FHWAO-IF-03-017 report prepared and regulated by the American Federal Highway Association for design purposes. It is inevitable to use this report in this project and other projects related to nailing. In this section, in order to show the capability of the presented model in assessing the stability of the pit, the probabilistic analysis related to the stabilization of the nailed wall has been investigated.

Statistical characteristics and characteristics of nails

The excavation depth in this example is 13 meters and the specifications of the construction materials are granular materials as shown in table (7).

Table 7. Soil resistance parameters

γ (in terms of 3 kN/m)	C (in terms of 2kN/m)	φ (in terms of angle)	
20	12	36	Soil characteristics

Effective parameters in the analysis of the stability of gables include: parameters of shear resistance (adhesion and internal friction angle), pore water pressure, specific weight, sliding surface resistance, surface loads and the like. In this research, three soil resistance parameters namely: c, ϕ and γ are considered as sources of uncertainty. Normal distribution was used for ϕ and γ parameters, but log normal distribution was used for adhesion to prevent the creation of negative random numbers. Also, the specifications of the statistical parameters are considered according to tables (8).

Table 8. Geotechnical parameters

Standard deviation	Coefficient of variation (%)	Average	Soil characteristics
1.4	7	20	γ (in terms of 3 kN/m)
4.8	40	12	C (in terms of 2kN/m)
3.6	10	36	φ (in angle)

Also, the probability distribution function related to the three parameters c, ϕ and γ which is selected according to table (8) is given in figures (14), (15) and (16).

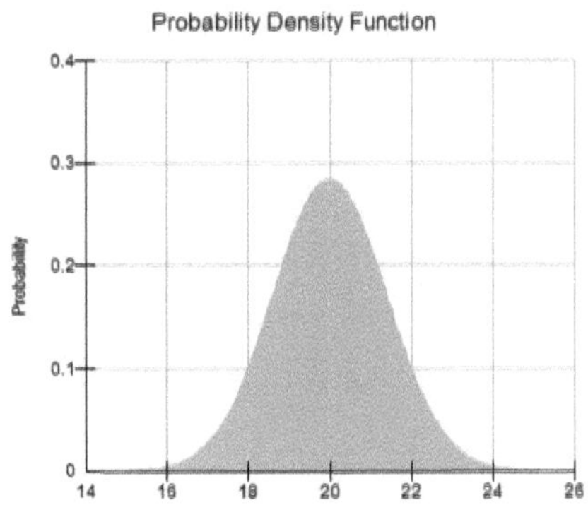

Figure 14. Normal distribution of specific gravity

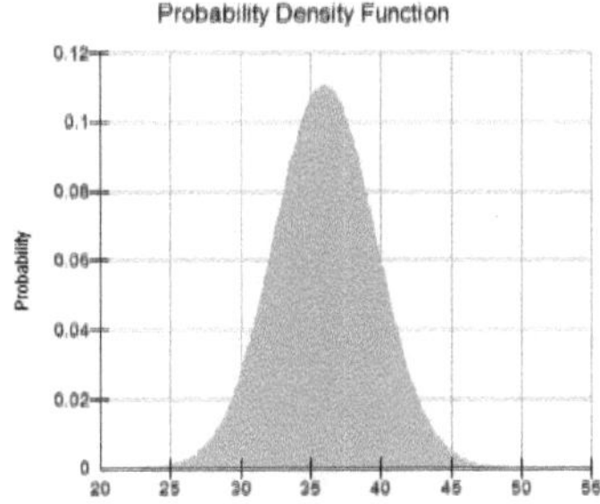

Figure 15. Normal distribution of internal friction angle

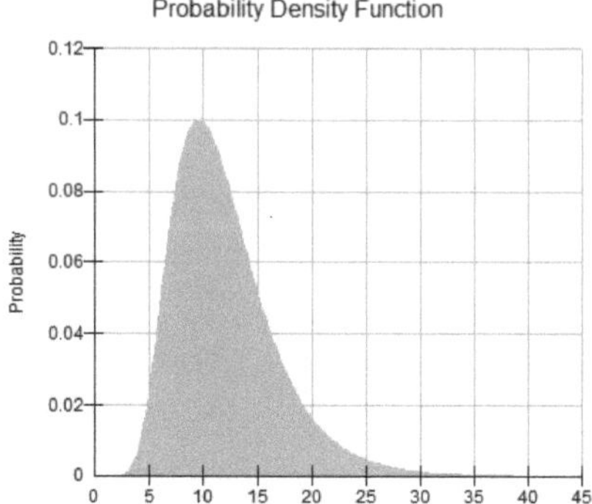

Figure 16. Log normal distribution of adhesion

The maximum and minimum values of the input parameters are considered to be 5 times the standard deviation on the sides of the average. With this assumption, more than 99.995% of the area under the curve of the normal density function is covered, which is enough accuracy for common engineering projects. To allocate the overhead on the wall, it is necessary to visit the place and the location of the nearby structures. If the exact value of existing overheads is not available, the values recommended in the FHWA regulations should be used. The amount recommended in this regulation is one ton per square meter for each floor of the building, which is equivalent to 10 kilopascals. Due to the presence of a 5-story building on the desired wall, the overhead allocated on this wall is 50 kilopascals.

Also, in this project, the nails are embedded in the wall according to the specifications of Table (9) with a horizontal distance of 1.5 meters and a vertical distance of 2.5 meters from each other.

Table 9. Specifications of inserted nails

Slip resistance of soil and grout (kPa)	Angle to the horizon (degrees)	Length of nails (m)	Injection hole diameter (cm)	Stud diameter (cm)	Row
200	15	8	12	32	1
200	15	7	12	32	2
200	15	6	12	32	3
200	15	5	12	32	4

The number of iterations and probability of failure in the Monte Carlo method

According to the materials mentioned in the previous chapter, the lowest number of repetitions of the Monte Carlo method with the selection of the standard deviation of 1.645 and the confidence level of 90% and the number of random variables in this study is according to the following relationship:

$$N = \left(\frac{d^2}{4(1-\varepsilon)^2} \right)^m = \left(\frac{1.645^2}{4(1-0.9)^2} \right)^3 = 309610$$

In the analysis, the number of Monte Carlo repetitions is considered equal to 310,000 repetitions.

By performing repeated calculations and calculating the confidence factor in each step, the frequency chart of the confidence factor is shown in figure (17). As can be seen in the figure, the frequency diagram is completely continuous and follows the normal probability distribution function.

As mentioned earlier, the probability of failure is equal to the level under the probability density function diagram (PDF) of the confidence factor in the range of answers smaller than one. The level below the probability density function diagram is equal to the value of the cumulative probability density function (CDF) of the confidence coefficient. Figures (18) and (19) show how to calculate the probability of failure.

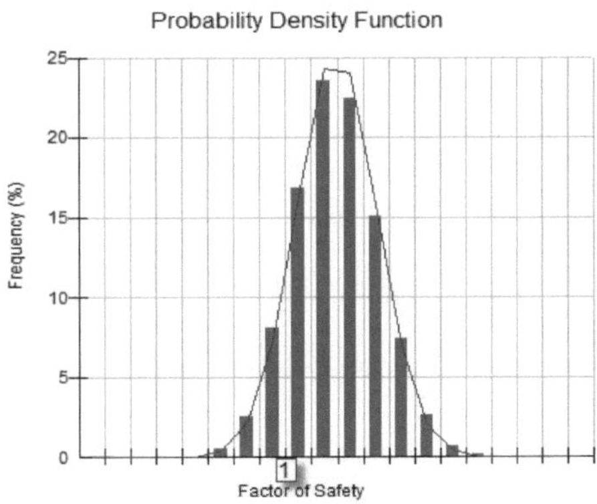

Figure 18. Confidence coefficient frequency chart

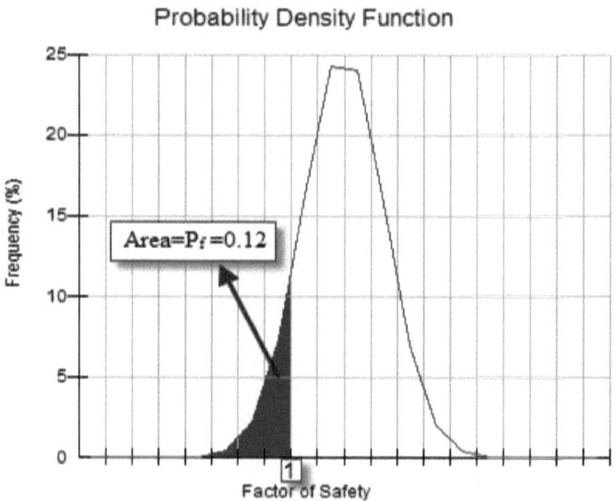

Figure 19. PDF function of reliability coefficient and how to calculate failure probability

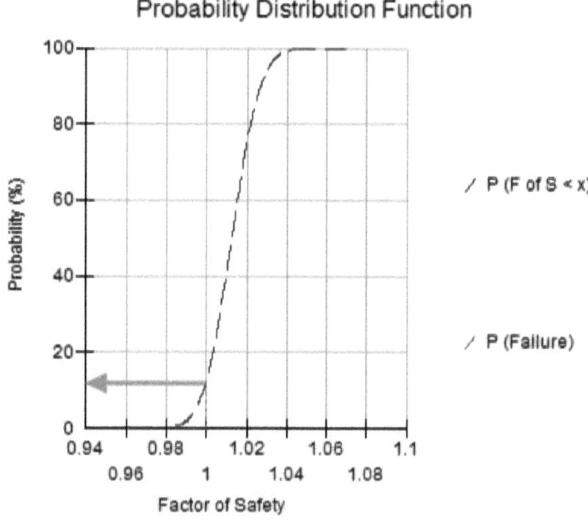

Figure 20. How to calculate the probability of failure from the CDF function?

Figures (19) and (20) respectively show the probability density function and the probability cumulative distribution function of the confidence factor obtained by using Monte Carlo simulation. The probability of failure is equal to the level under the reliability coefficient distribution function curve for values smaller than one, which is equivalent to a number like the reliability coefficient of one on the reliability coefficient cumulative distribution function curve.

After analyzing the number of 11,492 rupture levels with 310,000 repetitions, the obtained results indicate that the reliability index is 3.498 and the probability of rupture is 0.00839 percent, and the minimum and maximum confidence coefficients are 0.99214 and 1.095, respectively. Figures (21) and (22) show the reliability coefficient distribution diagram as well as the shape of the rupture surface.

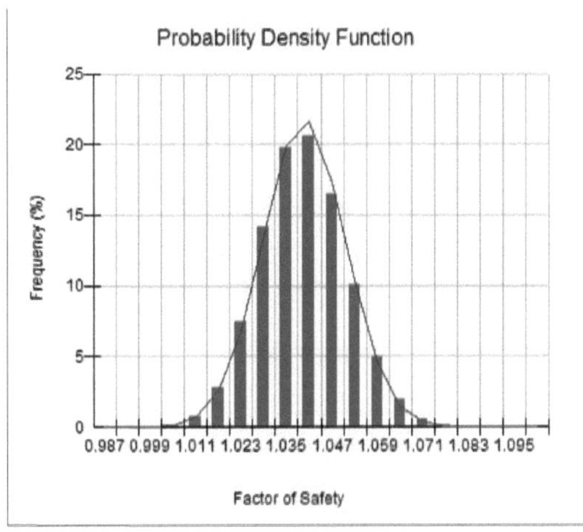

Figure 21. Probability density function of confidence coefficients

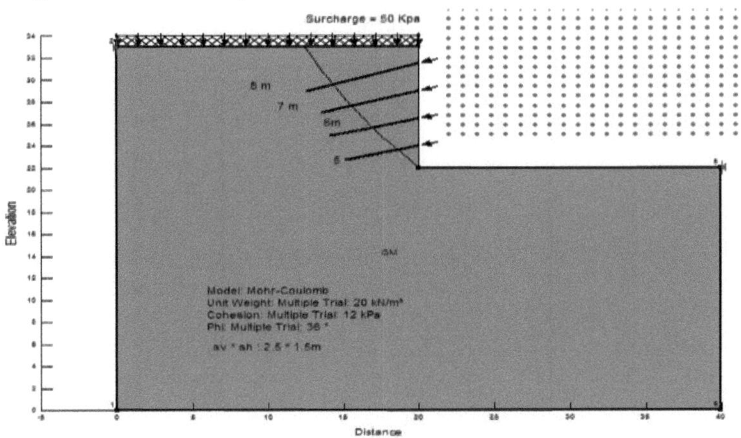

Figure 22. Critical rupture level

According to table and figure (22) (permissible values for breakage probability and reliability index) and the importance of the structure and expected performance level, we can discuss about the obtained results.

Examining the results of probabilistic analysis of pit wall stability using Monte Carlo method shows that:

- In the comparison of the deterministic and probabilistic analysis method of the rupture event, it can be seen that the confidence factor can be very probable, while in the deterministic design method, the results may be very conservative.

- Due to the uncertainties in solving the stability problems of reinforced and unreinforced slopes, such as the changeability of soil properties, simplifying assumptions in the analytical equations of various methods, the uncertainty of seismic coefficients, etc., usually engineers use deterministic methods and calculate a number as a safety factor, they cannot calculate and identify the existing risk level. But in the probabilistic method, we obtain probabilistic distributions for confidence coefficients. It is possible to obtain the probability of failure as well as the reliability of the design.

- According to the degree of importance of the structure as well as the values obtained for the reliability index and probability of failure, the performance level of the pit wall can be discussed and investigated. The performance level of the above example is within the tolerable performance range for structures with a low degree of importance, which naturally will not be ideal due to ignoring the implementation uncertainties.

- If the executive group is experienced and uses special equipment and arrangements, it can be said that the obtained reliability index indicates the economic nature of the project.

- Among the operations that can be done in order to increase the safety factor and reduce the risk in this project, we can mention the implementation of a steel pile under the column of the adjacent building. In fact, with this action, the stability of the desired pit is improved from a tolerable performance level to an acceptable performance level. Examining the effectiveness of control measures shows a noticeable increase in the safety factor due to the implementation of piles. So that in the redesign, the reliability factor increased to 1.202 and the possibility of failure was eliminated.

Sensitivity analysis

As mentioned, the type of probability distribution function is suggested for parameters whose coefficient of variation is less than 25%, normal distribution and if the coefficient of variation is more than 25%, log normal distribution. In the following, we will compare the effect of choosing the appropriate distribution for the input parameters. For this purpose, the distribution function of one of the input parameters is considered to be log-normal, and the distribution function of the other two parameters is considered to be normal, and the value of the target function (probability of failure) is calculated. The results are shown in table (10). As mentioned, the log-normal probability distribution function with a coefficient of variation greater than 25% is very close to the normal state. The results of the above table show that the value of the target function (probability of failure) has not changed by changing the distribution function of parameter C. But for the other 2 parameters whose coefficient of change is less than 25%, the results change with the change of the distribution function.

Table 10. The effect of the shape of the distribution function on the output values

Normal log			Normal	Distribution function
γ	φ	c	c,φ,γ	Input parameter
0.007	0.029	0.008	0.008	Possibility of failure
3.627	3.4	3.496	3.629	Reliability index
1.0407	1.0378	1.0396	1.0405	Average reliability coefficient
Normal	Normal	Normal	Normal	Confidence coefficient distribution

By studying the subject literature of the Monte Carlo method, one of the limitations of this method can be stated as the number of repetitions required for analysis. Based on the rules of probability, the number of repetitions required is obtained from equation 2-4. Although achieving this high number of repetitions is possible due to the hardware power of existing computers, but due to the desired accuracy in geotechnical engineering, the number of these repetitions can be significantly reduced in applied studies.

In order to investigate this matter more closely, a sensitivity analysis has been performed with respect to the number of consecutive repetitions. The results of figure (23) and table (11) show that after about 300 thousand repetitions, there is no significant change in the results and it has converged with acceptable accuracy.

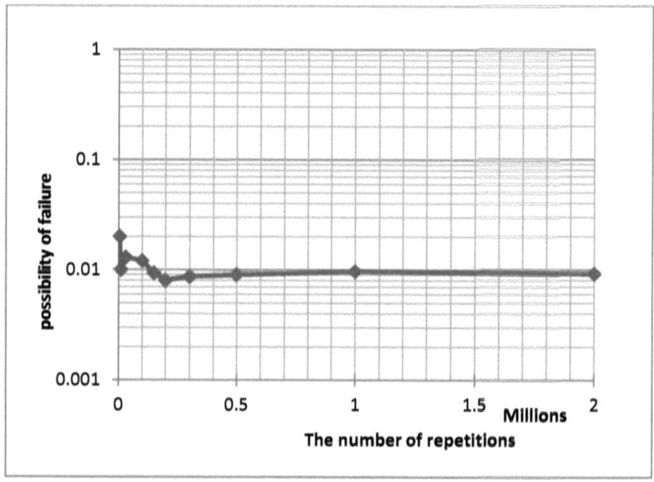

Figure 23. Checking the number of repetitions necessary to converge the probability of failure

Table 11. The effect of the number of repetitions on the Monte Carlo method

Average reliability coefficient	Capability index	Possibility of failure	The number of repetitions	Row
1.0396	3.487	0	2000	1
1.0395	3.453	0.02	5000	2
1.0394	3.459	0.01	10000	3
1.0396	3.487	0.01291	31000	4
1.0396	3.49	0.012	100000	5
1.0396	3.492	0.00934	150000	6
1.0396	3.496	0.008	200000	7
1.0396	3.499	0.00867	300000	8
1.0396	3.497	0.009	500000	9
1.0396	3.498	0.0097	1000000	10
1.0396	3.496	0.0092	2000000	11

The intensity of dependence of two correlation variables is defined. In general, the correlation coefficient changes between -1 and +1 and the relationship between two variables can be positive or negative. If x and y are two variable parameters with correlation coefficient r. If the correlation coefficient is +1, then there is a complete and direct correlation between the two parameters, and with the increase in the value of x, the value of y will definitely increase, and if the correlation coefficient is -1, then there is a complete and inverse correlation between the two parameters. The parameter is established and as x increases, the value of y decreases definitely.

In the case that $o < r < 1$, the correlation is incomplete and direct, and as the value of x increases, the value of y increases relatively. If $-1 < r < 0$, the correlation is incomplete and inverse, and as x increases, the value of y decreases relatively.

If r=0, it indicates no correlation. Correlation coefficients can be calculated empirically from statistical relationships. Laboratory studies on different types of soils show that the correlation of soil shear strength parameters (ϕ - c) is inverse and between -0.35

and -0.72. In this study, the correlation between ϕ - c parameters are inverse and equal to 0.5 (r=-0.5).

The Monte Carlo simulation method is based on the construction of random numbers based on the input parameters, and if the random parameters do not have a proper correlation, it can affect the results to a great extent and deviate them from the real values. In the studies conducted by Monte Carlo simulation, the effect of correlation between coefficients is generally ignored, while this factor in turn has an effect on the obtained answers. In this section, by assigning different correlation coefficients for adhesion-friction angle, the effect of correlation coefficient has been investigated. The results of this investigation are shown in figures (24) and (25).

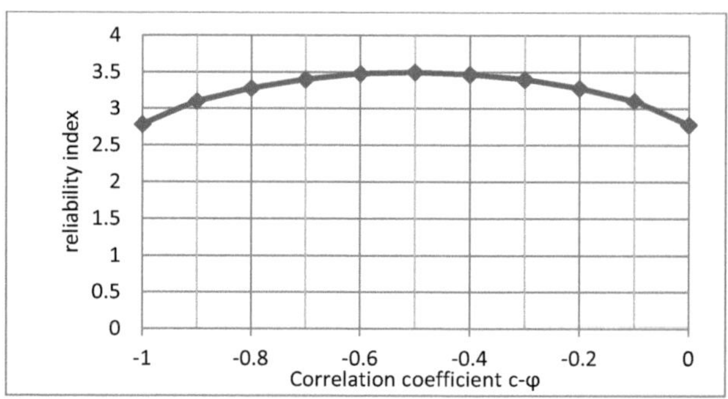

Figure 24. The effect of c-ϕ correlation coefficient on the reliability index

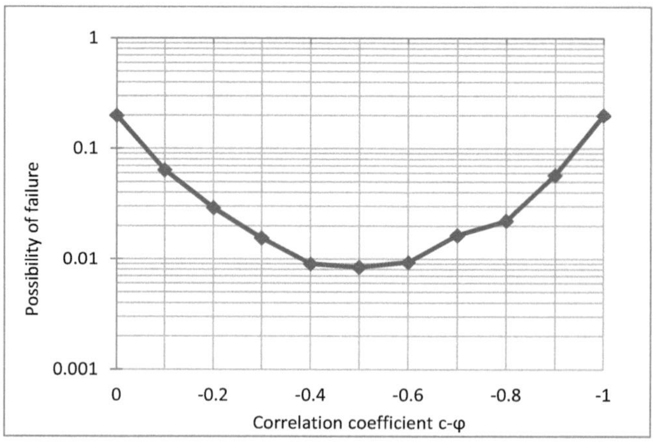

Figure 25. The effect of c-ϕ correlation coefficient on failure probability value

Parametric analysis

In the previous part, for sensitivity analysis, by increasing or decreasing the range of possible value changes for each parameter involved in the problem by one standard deviation, the failure probability changes were measured. Now the question may arise that maybe the behavior of the model is not linear to the change of the range of values of different input variables.

In other words, maybe if the range of input parameters values are changed by another factor of standard deviation instead of one standard deviation, different results will be obtained. Parametric analysis can be used to solve this doubt. The calculation process in parametric analysis is completely similar to sensitivity analysis, with the difference that the range of input statistical parameter values is done step by step and gradually. Among the issues that can be investigated by performing parametric analysis, the following can be mentioned:

- ❖ Controlling the logical trend of the model's response to the change of a parameter within an acceptable range (increasing or decreasing trend and consistent with sensitivity analysis).
- ❖ Investigating the linear or non-linear behavior of the model with respect to the changes of a parameter.
- ❖ Comparison and control of the slope of the model's response to the change of different parameters (the more sensitive parameter has a larger slope of changes).
- ❖ Examining the trend of changes in the slope of the model's response in the entire range of changes in different parameters.

Figure (26) shows the process of parametric analysis for the solved example. As can be seen in the figure, the range of values of each parameter has been changed by the standard deviation during ten steps while $\frac{1}{4}$ keeping the range of other parameters constant. In such a way that five steps have been associated with an increase in standard deviation and another five steps have been associated with a decrease in standard deviation, the reliability coefficient value has been calculated during each step.

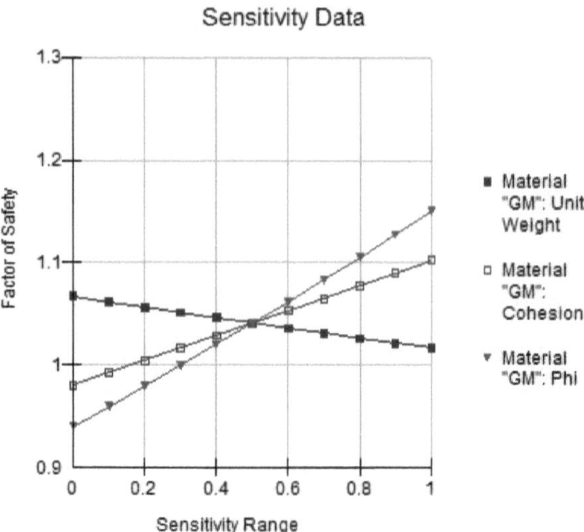

Figure 26. Parametric analysis of reliability coefficient based on step-by-step changes in the range of input parameters

Based on figure (26), with the increase in the range of the specific weight parameter, the reliability coefficient goes down, and with the increase in the range of the adhesion and friction angle values, it goes up. As can be seen in the figure, in every ten steps, the reliability coefficient has shown the highest sensitivity to the friction angle. According to the analyzes carried out in this section, it is recommended to pay attention to the following issues in the discussion of risk management of excavation projects and risk-based analyses:

➢ In probabilistic analysis, utmost care should be taken in choosing effective uncertainties and proportional distribution of each. For example, in choosing a normal distribution, care must be taken that the random numbers created for soil resistance parameters are not negative.

➢ The critical rupture level specified by the software must be chosen with special care. Because if the radius lines and drawing grid are not wide in the software, the selected rupture line is not necessarily the main rupture line, but the most critical rupture line in the defined range.

➢ It seems that according to the range of standard deviation for the soil resistance parameters and the overall standard deviation obtained for the confidence factor, it is possible to use the confidence factor as a tool for the safety index in excavation projects, along with probabilistic analysis as an indicator. Benefit for economic risk. In other words, by assuming a reliability coefficient higher than the reliability coefficients of the regulation, it can be said that the probability of failure and collapse of the pit in the performance level is much better than the acceptable performance level, but it entails an economic risk, which can be optimized with the risk analysis. in such a way that the level of safety and economic risk are in balance.

➢ Considering that the nailing method has been used in recent years in Tehran and some other big cities of Iran to stabilize the pit walls and is developing rapidly. It is suggested to compile the calculation and implementation instructions of this method, such as Cloture prepared in France, or instructions for trenching and securing using the truss method prepared by Tehran municipality.

Conclusion

The efficiency of using reliability techniques in engineering problems has been proven due to the possibility of more accurate examination of failure mechanisms compared to deterministic methods. On the other hand, in complex engineering problems with different boundary conditions, they are generally analyzed with numerical techniques. These methods provide good approximations of the limit equilibrium equation compared to other methods. Therefore, in order to be able to fully use the advantages of probabilistic analysis, it is necessary to use an advanced model and a suitable reliability technique. The use of finite element models and Monte Carlo simulation can be a suitable option for analyzing the reliability of geotechnical structures.

In this chapter, the analysis of reliability and probability of failure was discussed and investigated using the Monte Carlo simulation method. This chapter generally includes two parts, in the first part the risk assessment process and in the second part the feasibility of using the Monte Carlo simulation method in assessing the probability of failure of pits was presented. Also, in the second part, by describing an example and verifying it, the efficiency of this method to evaluate the probability of failure was tested. In addition to the high efficiency of the Monte Carlo simulation method, this case study confirmed the superiority of the reliability analysis method over deterministic analysis and showed that deterministic methods are not very reliable and engineering judgment using the deterministic method faces serious challenges.

Since there is no clear relationship between the reliability coefficient of deterministic methods and the probability of failure, and the use of reliability methods requires statistical information, programming and relatively high computational volume, it was attempted to use the results of the Monte Carlo simulation method to establish a logical relationship between the level performance of the structure and the possibility of failure.

Chapter V

Conclusions and Suggestions

The use of maximum density and the construction of basement floors is optional, but the complete stabilization of excavation walls and ensuring the safety of workers and neighbors is mandatory from a technical and legal point of view. The stability of pits is faced with uncertainties that must be properly considered in their design. Engineering judgment is always one of the most challenging issues in the geotechnical field, which is very complicated due to many uncertainties. In the past, engineering judgment was only based on experience, but the role of engineering judgment has changed in recent years due to advances in statistical models and reliability theories. In choosing geotechnical parameters and designing geotechnical structures, the geotechnical engineer must judge in such a way that the risks related to them are acceptable. Estimating the probability of rupture empirically is difficult, and reliability analysis can be an effective help.

The existence of uncertainties and their impact in design have been known for many years, and uncertainties are traditionally considered by choosing a confidence factor in design. In principle, determining the reliability coefficient is a function of the uncertainty in the applied loads, the errors of the analytical method used, geotechnical variables, ground conditions, and also the inaccuracy in the execution works, but a professional engineer does not go into the details of the uncertainty caused by various factors to choose the reliability coefficient. Relying on his general understanding of uncertainties, he chooses the confidence factor with engineering judgment. Analysis based on risk assessment is a subject that has recently attracted the attention of researchers due to the existence of uncertainties in geotechnical issues. Because the existence of uncertainties leads to unreliable designs. Therefore, the degree of uncertainty of the design and the risks caused by this design should be evaluated in order to reduce the number of damages by risk management. With the help of risk-based methods, the details of uncertainties and their factors can be studied.

Applying the reliability coefficient in the classical form has many problems. First, the reliability coefficient is not fixed and the minimum value of the proposed reliability coefficient depends on the type of problem. Second, there is no clear relationship between the reliability coefficient and the probability of breakage.

That is, choosing a large confidence factor does not always mean a significant reduction in the probability of breakage. Of course, engineering judgment is still needed in probabilistic studies and is used to choose the level of risk or the probability of acceptable rupture. In this thesis, failure probability analysis was investigated using the Monte Carlo simulation method and how to calculate the failure probability was shown by an example.

Results

Geotechnical projects carry many risks due to the existence of many uncertainties. In deterministic analysis methods based on traditional approaches, the best solution to reduce or eliminate risk is to increase confidence coefficients and conservatively select input parameters which in many cases is more than the required amount and in some cases it is less than that. In other words, there are two basic problems in these methods: Firstly, increasing the reliability coefficients increases costs and thus leads to economic risk. Secondly, the exact amount of conservatism is not available for structures with different degrees of importance.

In other words, as the importance coefficient of the structure increases, we do not have any criteria for choosing the confidence coefficient corresponding to that structure. In fact, it is not possible to determine the exact impact of uncertainty on the safety of pits. If the analysis and design is done considering the uncertainties in the system, the evaluation and checking of the statistical characteristics of the outputs of a system is expressed as a function of the uncertain parameters effective in it. This means that the impact of the uncertainty of the input parameters will be applied to the output values. This method has two advantages, firstly, the uncertainties are managed in a logical way in the design and calculations, and the sensitivity of the different design variables is accurately analyzed or determined. Second, these methods have a more logical basis than the decision-making of completely deterministic analyses.

The general results of this thesis can be summarized as follows:

➢ The probability density functions calculated for the reliability coefficient have a normal distribution.

➢ Most soil parameters follow a normal distribution, except in cases where it is not possible to use a normal distribution.

➢ The Monte Carlo simulation method is one of the methods that uses non-deterministic and random inputs to estimate the distribution of outputs and determines the relevant risk. Using this method, it is possible to calculate the probability of failure and the reliability index, which are actually indicators of risk assessment.

➢ The design based on risk assessment can cover some of the limitations of the certainty factor. Design based on risk assessment means trying to quantify the inherent uncertainties of an engineering problem and how to deal with them. Quantitative risk assessment includes risk analysis, risk assessment and risk management.

➢ Simultaneous attention to risk analysis and risk control is called risk management. Risk control is one of the important parts of risk management, which includes the examination of risk exposure options, including risk reduction, risk acceptance, or risk avoidance. Another result of risk-based design is quantifying the reliability of the structure, which is called the reliability index.

➢ Due to the fact that risk-based design is in the stage of evolution, it is currently more common to use this approach as an auxiliary tool next to deterministic methods. In fact, the quantitative risk assessment method does not replace the definitive and accepted existing methods, but instead of the conventional qualitative expressions such as "Safe" and "Unsafe", it deals with the numerical expression of the risk in a system.

➢ The effect of the correlation coefficient between the parameters is very important on the results, so this effect should be considered in the simulation of the parameters.

- Comparing the results of deterministic analysis and reliability shows that the use of deterministic method in the design of highly important structures is not accurate enough and engineering judgment using the results of deterministic method is simply not possible.

- The results of sensitivity analysis and parametric analysis of the presented model to evaluate the probability of failure show that the presented model predicts well the uncertainty in the parameters of the problem. In other words, the results of sensitivity analysis and parametric analysis show the correct performance of the presented model with respect to the change of different parameters.

- Based on the results of the sensitivity analysis of the presented model, the friction angle parameter has the highest and the specific weight parameter has the lowest effect and sensitivity on the value of the confidence factor.

- The results of the parametric analysis show that the effect of all three parameters on the reliability coefficient is almost linear.

Suggestions for future research

Considering the drawbacks of deterministic methods and the effectiveness of probabilistic methods mentioned in this thesis, this thesis presented the calculation of probability of failure using Monte Carlo simulation as a factor in risk management and control in excavation projects. Since the use of probabilistic methods in geotechnical designs is in its initial stages, in order to complete and develop this method, it is necessary to continue studies in the following fields:

- As it was said in today's studies, probabilistic methods and risk-based methods are used as auxiliary tools alongside conventional methods, it is expected that this design method will gradually replace conventional methods.

- Using the Monte Carlo simulation method, it is possible to calculate the probability of failure, but the criteria for the acceptable probability for structures with different degrees of importance are not yet clearly defined, and it is necessary to carry out additional studies in this field in order to make a decision. Facilitate measures related to risk management.

➢ In this thesis, the evaluation of the probability of failure of pits was investigated by considering the parametric uncertainties. Considering the uncertainty of the model can also be a good field for future research.

➢ Design based on structure performance is a new method based on the analysis of events based on different performance levels. The main part of the design is based on the function of calculating the probability of events, which is described in this thesis. Based on this, the design based on the performance of the structure can be very practical.

➢ Taking into account different rupture scenarios and drawing a tree of events for the possibility of failure, it is possible to analyze the risk of excavations. Risk analysis makes it possible to calculate the amount of risks economically and judge between different scenarios.

➢ As stated in the third chapter, reliability analysis methods can be divided into three categories: Analytical, approximate, and simulation methods. Comparing these methods can have significant results.

➢ The use of random field theory to model the heterogeneous soil environment can provide a suitable analysis of the probability of failure.

References

Akbari Hamed, Ardalan, Moghadaripour, Mohammad. and Rahmani, Iraj (2011). Reliability analysis of nailed walls using probabilistic Monte Carlo method. Proceedings of the 2nd Reliability Engineering Conference. Tehran, Aerospace Research Institute.

Taghizadeh Ghahi, Ezatollah (2008). Stabilization of deep excavation walls by nailing method in urban areas. Fine Arts Journal, No. 35, Fall 2017, pp. 51-61.

Kasebzadeh, J. (2013). Evaluation of soil liquefaction potential by reliability analysis method. Master's Thesis in Civil Engineering - Soil and Foundation Mechanics, Faculty of Water and Environmental Engineering, Shahid Beheshti University.

Manafi Gharabaei, S.M. (2011). Investigating the instability of the earthen dam body in safety management using risk assessment. Master's Thesis in Civil Engineering -Soil and Foundation Mechanics, Faculty of Water and Environmental Engineering, Shahid Abbaspur University of Water and Electrical Engineering.

Manafi Gharabaei, Seyyed Massoud., Noorzad, Ali., Mahdavifar, Mohammad Reza. and Bagheri Khalili, Faezeh (2011). Assessment of the instability risk of the earthen dam body by Monte Carlo method (case study: Dosti Dam). The first international conference and the third national conference on dams and hydropower plants. Tehran, http://www.civilica.com/Paper-NCHP03-NCHP03_400.html

Abramson, L. (2002). Slope Stability and Stabilization Methods. McGraw-Hill, New York.

Ang, A. S., Tang, A. H. (1984). Probability Concepts in Engineering Planning and Design. Inc, New York, vol. vol. II, 1984.

Aven, T., Vinnem, J. E. (2007). Risk Management Principles and Methods-Review and Discussion. Risk Management: With Applications from the Offshore Petroleum Industry, 19-75.

Baecher, G. B. (1987). Geotechnical Risk Analysis User's Guide (No. FHWA/RD-87-011).

Baecher, G. B., Christian, J. T. (2005). Reliability and Statistics in Geotechnical Engineering. John Wiley & Sons, New York.

Box, G. E., Muller, M. E. (1958). A Note on the Generation of Random Normal Deviates. Mathematical Statistics, Vol. 29, pp. 610-611.

Cao, Z. (2012). Probabilistic Approaches for Geotechnical Site Characterization and Slope Stability Analysis.

Cardenas, I. C., Halman, J. I. M., & Al-Jibouri, S. H. (2009). An Uncertainty-based Framework to Support Decision-making in Geotechnical Engineering Projects.

Chandler, D. S., (1996). Monte Carlo Simulation to Evaluate Slope Stability. Conference Proceeding on Uncertainty in the Geologic Environment, Wisconsin, Vol. 1, pp. 474-493.

Chowdhury, j. (2009). Geotechnical Risk Assessment and Hazard Management Guidelines. Principal Engineer Geotechnical.

Chowdhury, R.N., (1987), Practical Aspects of Probabilistic Studies for Slopes, Soil Slope Instability and Stabilization, Sydney, pp. 299-304.

Chowdhury, R.N., Xu, D.W. (1995), Geotechnical System Reliability of Slopes. Reliability Engineering and System Safety. Vol.47, pp. 141-151.

Christian, J. T., Ladd, C. C., & Baecher, G. B. (1994). Reliability Applied to Slope Stability Analysis. Journal of Geotechnical Engineering, 120 (12), 2180-2207.

Dai, F. C., Lee, C. F., & Ngai, Y. Y. (2002). Landslide Risk Assessment and Management: an Overview. Engineering geology, 64 (1), 65-87.

Danka, J. (2011). Probability of failure calculation of dikes based on Monte Carlo simulation. In Geotechnical Engineering: New Horizons: Proceedings of the 21st European Young Geotechnical Engineers' Conference, Rotterdam 181p. IOS Press.

Duncan, J. M. (2000). Factors of Safety and Reliability in Geotechnical Engineering. Journal of Geotechnical and Geo Environmental Engineering, Vol. 126, No. 4, pp. 307-316.

Ergun, M. U. (2008). Deep Excavations. Electronic Journal of Geotechnical Engineering, Available at: www. ejge. com/Bouquet08/UfukErgun_ppr. pdf.

Fell, R. (1994). Landslide Risk Assessment and Acceptable Risk. Canadian Geotechnical Journal, 31 (2), 261-272.

Fell, R., & Hartford, D. (1997). Landslide Risk Management. Balkema, 51-110.

Fell, R., Ho, K. K. S., Lacasse, S., Leroi, E. (2005, May). State of the Art Paper 1-A framework for landslide risk assessment and management. Proceedings of the International Conference on Landslide Risk Management, Vancouver, Canada, Vol. 31.

Fenton, G. A., Griffiths, D. V. (2008). Risk Assessment in Geotechnical Engineering 480 p. New York: John Wiley & Sons.

Ferris, G., Samchek, A., and Isherwood, A. (2003) Geotechnical Risk Assessment: Estimating Slope Failure Probability. New Pipeline Technologies, Security, and Safety: pp. 1252-1260.

FHWA. (2003). Geotechnical Engineering Circular No. 7–soil nail walls. Report FHWA0-IF-03-017.

Fredlund, D.G., Krahn, J. (1977), Comparison of Slope Stability Methods of Analysis. Canadian Geotechnical Journal Vo1.14, No. 3, pp. 429-439.

Gerco, V.R. (1996), Efficient Monte Carlo technique for locating critical slip surface. Journal of Geotechnical Engineering. Vol.122, No. 7, July, pp. 517-525.

Griffiths, D. V., Fenton, G. (2007). Probabilistic Methods in Geotechnical Engineering, Springer Wien New York, USA.

Griffiths, D. V., Fenton, G. A. (2004). Probabilistic slope stability analysis by finite elements. Journal of Geotechnical and Geo Environmental Engineering,130(5), 507-518.

Hammond, C. J., Prellwitz, R. W. & Miller, S. M. (1991). Landslide Hazard Assessment Using Monte Carlo Simulation, Proceedings of the Sixth International Symposium on Landslide, Rotterdam, Vol. 2, pp. 959-964.

Harr, M. (1987). Reliability-Based Design in Civil Engineering, McGraw-Hill Book Company, USA.

Hasofer A. M. and Lind. N. C. (1974). Exact and invariant second-moment code format. Journal of the Engineering Mechanics Division, Vol. 100, pp. 111-121.

Hoek, E. (1998). Factor of safety and probability of failure. Rock Engineering, Course notes, 105-114.

Jaksa, M. B., Kaggwa, W. S., Fenton, G. A., & Poulos, H. G. (2003). A framework for quantifying the reliability of geotechnical investigations. In 9th International Conference on the Application of Statistics and Probability in Civil Engineering, pp. 1285-1291.

Jones, A. L., Kramer, S. L., & Arduino, P. (2002). Estimation of uncertainty in geotechnical properties for performance-based earthquake engineering. Pacific Earthquake Engineering Research Center, College of Engineering, University of California.

Juang, C. H., Jhi, Y. Y., & Lee, D. H. (1998). Stability analysis of existing slopes considering uncertainty. Engineering Geology, 49(2), 111-122.

Krahn, J., 2004, Stability Modeling with SLOPE/W, GEO-SLOPE/W International, Ltd., Alberta, Canada.

Kulhawy, F. H. (1993). On the evaluation of static soil properties. McGraw-Hill Book Company.

Kulhawy, F. H., Phoon, K. K., & Prakoso, W. A. (2000). Uncertainty in basic properties of geomaterials. Proceedings of GeoEng2000, Melbourne.

Lacasse, S., Nadim, F. (1997). Uncertainties in Characterizing Soil Properties, Publikasjon-Norges Geotekniske Institutt, Vol. 201, pp. 49-75.

Lacasse, S., Nadim, F. (1998). Risk and Reliability in Geotechnical Engineering. In Proceedings Fourth International Conference on Case Histories in Geotechnical Engineering, St Louis, Missouri, March, pp. 9-12.

Lacasse, S., Nadim, F., & HoΦeg, K. (2012) Risk Assessment and Mitigation in Geo-Practice. Geotechnical Engineering State of the Art and Practice: pp. 729-764.

Lo, S. C. R. (Ed.). (1993). Probabilistic methods in geotechnical engineering: proceedings of the Conference on Probabilistic Methods in Geotechnical Engineering, Canberra, Australia, 10-12 February 1993. AA Balkema.

Low, B. K. (2003). Practical probabilistic slope stability analysis. Proceedings, soil and rock America, 2, 2777-84.

Low, B. K. Tang, W. H. (1997). Efficient reliability evaluation using spreadsheet. Engineering mechanics, Vol. 123 (7), pp. 749-752.

Mejstrik, M., Degebrodt, P., Rackwitz, F., Savidis, S. (2008, October). Development and Practical Adoption of an Internet-Based Platform for Geotechnical Engineering Projects. In Proc. 12th International Conference of the International Association for Computer Methods and Advances in Geo mechanics (IACMAG), pp. 1-6.

Morgan, G.C., (1991). Quantification of risks from slope hazards. Open File Report No. 1992 -15, Geological Survey of Canada.

Morgenstern, N.R. and Price, V.E., (1965). The analysis of the stability of general slip surfaces, Geo technique, Vol. 15, No. 1, pp. 79-93.

Mostyn, G.R., (1998). Course notes from Quantitative Risk Assessment for Soil and Rock Slopes, University of New South Wales Short Course.

Ou, C. Y. (2006). Deep excavation: theory and practice. Taylor & Francis.

Phoon, K. K. (2004). Towards reliability-based design for geotechnical engineering. Special lecture for Korean Geotechnical Society, Seoul.

Phoon, K. K. (2008). "Reliability Based Design in Geotechnical Engineering", Taylor and Francis, USA and Canada.

Phoon, K. K., Kulhawy, F. H. (1999). Characterization of geotechnical variability. Canadian Geotechnical Journal, 36 (4), 612-624.

Puller, M. (2003). Deep excavations: a practical manual. Thomas Telford.

Rajabalinejad, M. (2009). "Reliability method for Finite Element Models", IOS Press. Netherland.

Grocott, G. (1998). Quantitative Assessment Methods for Determining Slope Stability Risk in the Building Industry. Institute of Geological & Nuclear Sciences Information Series, (45), 104.

Rosenblueth, E. (1975). Point Estimates for Probability Moments. Proceedings of the National Academy of Sciences, Vol. 72, pp. 3812-3814.

Savidis, S.A., Rackwitz, F. (2007). Risk Management in Geotechnical Engineering

Projects by Means of an Internet-Based Information and Cooperation Platform. First International Symposium on Geotechnical Safety & Risk. Shanghai, Tongji University, China.

Schweckendiek, T., Calle, E. O. F. (2010). A Factor of Safety for Geotechnical Characterization. In Proc. of the Seventeenth Southeast Asian Geotechnical Conference (17SEAGC)–Geo-Engineering for Natural Hazard Mitigation and Sustainable Development, Vol. 2, pp. 227-230.

Shen, H. (2012). Non-deterministic analysis of slope stability based on numerical simulation (Doctoral dissertation).

Sho-Ho, D. Wang, O. (1992). Reliability Analysis in Geotechnical Engineering. Taylor and Francis.

Silva, F., Lambe, T. W., & Marr, W. A. (2008). Probability and risk of slope failure. Journal of geotechnical and geo environmental engineering, 134 (12), 1691-1699.

Silva, F., Lambe, T., Marr, W. (2008), "Probability and Risk of Slope Failure." J. Geo tech. Geo environ. Eng., 134(12), 1691-1699.

Spencer, E., 1967, A method of analysis of the stability of embankments assuming parallel inter-slice forces, Geo technique, Vol. 17, No. 1, pp. 11-26.

Stanković, J. N., Filipović, S., Rajković, R., Obradović, L., & Kovačević, R. Risk and Reliability Analysis of Slope Stability-Deterministic and Probabilistic Method.

Sullivan, T. D. (2006). Pit slope design and risk–A view of the current state of the art. International Symposium on Stability of Rock Slopes in Open Pit Mining and Civil Engineering. The South African Institute of Mining and Metallurgy. Symposium Series, Vol. 544.

TC17, (2004). Soil Nailing Technical Report Is SMFE FHWA-RD-84-93 Excavations & Soil Nailing of Highway Slopes.

U.S. Army Corps of Engineers, 1995, Introduction to probability and reliability methods for use in geotechnical engineering. Engineering Technical Letter 1110-2-547, U.S. Army Corps of Engineers, Washington, D.C.

Van Staveren, M. T. (2009). Extending to geotechnical risk management. Geo risk, 3 (3), pp. 174-183.

Vanmarcke, E.H., 1977, Reliability of earth slopes, Journal of the Geotechnical Engineering Division, Vol. 103, pp. 1247–1265.

Wang, Y., Cao, Z., & Au, S. K. (2010). Practical reliability analysis of slope stability by advanced Monte Carlo simulations in a spreadsheet. Canadian Geotechnical Journal, 48 (1), 162-172.

Wang, Y., Cao, Z., Au, S. K., & Wang, Q. (2009, June). Reliability analysis of a benchmark problem for slope stability. In Proceedings of Second International Symposium on geotechnical safety and risk. Gifu, Japan (pp. 89-93).

Whitman, V.W., 1984, Evaluating calculated risk in geotechnical engineering, Journal of Geotechnical Engineering, No. 110, pp. 145–188.

Wolff, T.F., 1996, Probabilistic slope stability in theory and practice, Proceedings of Uncertainty '96, Vol. 2, pp. 419–433.

Worley Consultants Ltd, 1987: Slope Stability Assessment at Building Sites. Building Research Association of New Zealand. BRANZ Study Report SR4. Judgeford.

Printed by Books on Demand GmbH, Norderstedt / Germany